Social Indicators Research Series

Volume 7

General Editor:

ALEX C. MICHALOS
University of Northern British Columbia,
Prince George, Canada

Editors:

ED DIENER
University of Illinois, Champaign, U.S.A.

WOLFGANG GLATZER
J.W. Goethe University, Frankfurt am Main, Germany

TORBJORN MOUM
University of Oslo, Norway

JOACHIM VOGEL
Central Bureau of Statistics, Stockholm, Sweden

RUUT VEENHOVEN
Erasmus University, Rotterdam, The Netherlands

This new series aims to provide a public forum for single treatises and collections of papers on social indicators research that are too long to be published in our journal *Social Indicators Research*. Like the journal, the book series deals with statistical assessments of the quality of life from a broad perspective. It welcomes the research on a wide variety of substantive areas, including health, crime, housing, education, family life, leisure activities, transportation, mobility, economics, work, religion and environmental issues. These areas of research will focus on the impact of key issues such as health on the overall quality of life and vice versa. An international review board, consisting of Ruut Veenhoven, Joachim Vogel, Ed Diener, Torbjorn Moum and Wolfgang Glatzer, will ensure the high quality of the series as a whole.

The titles published in this series are listed at the end of this volume.

MEASURING AND MONITORING
CHILDREN'S WELL-BEING

MEASURING AND MONITORING CHILDREN'S WELL-BEING

by

ASHER BEN-ARIEH

Associate Director,
Israel National Council for the Child

NATALIE HEVENER KAUFMAN

Professor, Institute for Families and Neighbourhoods,
Clemson University

ARLENE BOWERS ANDREWS

Director, Institute for Families in Society,
University of South Carolina

ROBERT M. GOERGE

Associate Director,
Chapin Hall Center for Children at the University of Chicago

BONG JOO LEE

Research Fellow,
Chapin Hall Center for Children at the University of Chicago

J. LAWRENCE ABER

Director,
National Center for Children in Poverty,
Columbia University

KLUWER ACADEMIC PUBLISHERS
DORDRECHT / BOSTON / LONDON

A C.I.P. Catalogue record for this book is available from the Library of Congress.

Measuring and monitoring children's well-being / Asher Ben-Arieh ... [et al.] ; with a
preface by Helmut Wintersberger.
    p. cm. -- (Social indicators research series ; v. 7)
    Includes bibliographical references and index.
    ISBN 0-7923-6789-8 (hardbound : alk. paper)
    1. Child welfare--Evaluation. 2. Child psychology. 3. Children's rights. 4. Quality of
life. I. Ben-Arieh, Asher, 1963- II. Series.

HV713 .M43 2001
62.6--dc21

                                                                        00-067184

ISBN 0-7923-6789-8

Published by Kluwer Academic Publishers,
P.O. Box 17, 3300 AA Dordrecht, The Netherlands.

Sold and distributed in North, Central and South America
by Kluwer Academic Publishers,
101 Philip Drive, Norwell, MA 02061, U.S.A.

In all other countries, sold and distributed
by Kluwer Academic Publishers,
P.O. Box 322, 3300 AH Dordrecht, The Netherlands.

Printed on acid-free paper

Printed and bound in the Netherlands.

This book is dedicated to our partners:
Hamutal Ben-Arieh, David Whiteman, Stuart Andrews, Lisa
Karron, Kyung Mi Lee and Christine B. Pendry.

It is also dedicated to our children: Oren and Nitzan, Carrollee
and Athey, Emily and Brook, Talia, Seoyun and Seoho, Nick and
Emma.

They are the reason for our well-being.

The Authors

Table of Contents

Preface

Today, any regular newspaper reader is likely to be exposed to reports on manifold forms of (physical, emotional, sexual) child abuse on the one hand, and abnormal behavior, misconduct or offences of children and minors on the other hand. Occasionally reports on children as victims and children as offenders may appear on the same issue or even the same page. Rather seldom the more complex and largely hidden phenomena of structural hostility or indifference of society with a view to children are being dealt with in the press. Such fragmentary, ambiguous, incoherent or even contradictory perception of children in modern society indicates that, firstly, there is a lack of reliable information on modern childhood, and secondly, children are still treated as a comparatively irrelevant population group in society.

This conclusion may be surprising in particular when drawn at the end of *The Century of the Child* proclaimed by Ellen Key as early as 1902. Actually, there exist unclarities and ambiguities about the evolution of childhood in the last century not only in public opinion, but also in scientific literature. While De Mause with his psycho-historic model of the evolution of childhood, comprising different stages from infanticide, abandonment, ambivalence, intrusion, socialisation to support, underlines the continuous improvement of the condition of childhood throughout history and thus rather confirms Key's expectations, Ariès, with his social history of childhood, seems to hold a more culturally pessimistic view. Much depends on the standpoint: whether we refer to the situation of children world-wide or to a comparatively small number of children living in the most developed countries; whether we refer primarily to the development of parent-child relations or to the evolution of generational relations between children and adults at the level of society; whether we are prepared to acknowledge progress already along with identification of problems and formulation of rights, or whether we recognise it only along with the solution of problems and the transformation of rights into realities.

In my view, major achievements have been made in the last century in terms of building awareness, in particular under the guidance of NGOs; in research in both traditional childhood sciences as psychology and paediatrics, but also new disciplines like sociology of childhood and children; and finally the UN-Convention on the Rights of the Child as well as related legal reforms and political declarations at national and international levels are to be mentioned in this connection. On the other hand much is left for the 21st century with a view to improving the situation of children in developed societies as well as world-wide. Therefore today, the gap between aspirations and realities might even be bigger than a century ago.

The present volume on "Measuring and Monitoring Children's Well-Being" is to be interpreted in the context of the tensions caused by this gap. Even more, its object of study is precisely the gap between aspirations and realities in the well-being of children, and its aim providing tools for reducing tensions and bridging realities and expectations. The book deals with the interrelations between knowledge, information and data on one side, and practices, policies and power relations on the other. "Information in general and data in particular have the power to shape and influence policy and services" (chapter 1, p. 1). One could add, that not only information implies power, but also vice versa, power influences also the shaping of information, not only in the sense of using or retaining it, but already in the process of generating and collecting.

"In what has been called the Information Age, we know surprisingly little about the state of our children." This statement - contained right in the beginning of chapter 1 (p.1) - seems to be contradicted by the content of chapter 2 giving an overview of existing efforts of monitoring and measuring children's well-being all around the world. This overview contains an extended number of single-, multi- and integrated-issue reports; on the whole or segments of the child population at global, regional, national and local levels. The UNICEF Annual State of the World's Children Report could here be mentioned just as one, though prominent example.

However, the contradiction mentioned above is only an apparent one, because the available information on children is usually selective and adult-biased in various ways. Reports and data on families, schools, as well as child care and welfare institutions are mostly not reports or data on children; even if children may be a crucial component of those institutions, children are generally not the unit of observation used. Children are often considered as objects and not as subjects, persons and citizens. Usually reports on children take more interest in a developmental and socialisation perspective, in children's prospects as future adults, than in their status here and now. And too frequently there is an emphasis on children at risk as well as on pathological phenomena like mortality, morbidity, child abuse and juvenile delinquency, while the basic conditions of childhood affecting the child population at large are widely neglected.

To eliminate those shortcomings, in the present book childhood is being considered as a stage in itself and children as a population group of its own, emphasis is being placed on positive indicators, and children are being made the unit of observation (chapter 3). This research orientation, however, does not at all lead to a monolithic theory and methodology. There is still sufficient space for diversity of approaches, as for instance actor oriented child research as well as structure oriented childhood research, or objective as well as subjective perceptions of children's well-being.

The title of the book contains also the term of "children's well-being", a concept, although phonetically similar to the more familiar concept of "child welfare", is wider and open to other, more authentic interpretations. In this sense, it may well be, that governments and other organisations pay considerable attention to what they believe to be child welfare, while there are poor outcomes in terms of (objective or subjective) well-being of children. It was therefore necessary to create a new structure for elaborating and presenting indicators of children's well-being. As a result, the set of indicators proposed for monitoring and measuring the well-being of children (chapter 5) is organised in the frame of five substantive domains, which are discussed in chapter 4.

Relatively new are the domains of children's activities, covering children's engagement in work, play, consumption, social interactions and other activities that are analogous to adult activities yet qualitatively different; as well as of children's economic resources and contributions, comprising the essential aspects of generational distributive justice and generational division of labour.

Already more familiar sounds the domain of civic life skills including development of social and civic responsibilities, acquisition and exercise of self-expression, knowledge about and participation in legal and civic activities, understanding and respect for the rights of others, and genuine tolerance of diversity. This domain reflects predominantly the participatory content of the UN Convention on the Rights of the Child, which is generally seen as its most innovative part and currently debated in a number of governmental and non-governmental, national and international organizations, as for instance the European Union, the Council of Europe and the European Children's Network.

Those three domains are rounded up by two more traditional domains, namely children's personal life skills, in the sense of skills to contribute to their own well-being, including self-esteem and assertiveness as well as the capacity to work; and finally safety and physical status, commonly thought of as the most basic component of well-being.

The last chapters of the book are dedicated to the presentation and application of indicators of children's well-being. A set of some 50 indicators, covering the five domains, was developed in the context of the international project. The outcome of this exercise is contained in chapter's 5 and 6.

In chapters 7 and 8 the debate on research and action/policies is being resumed. What are the benefits of indicators for improving the situation of children at the community and macro-political levels? Which properties should indicators have, in order to develop the desired outcomes?

Measuring and monitoring processes at the community level, in order to be effective, have to fulfill a number of conditions among them "inclusivity and cultural relevance, reliability and validity, feasibility, repetition, facilitation of interpretation, and utility" (chapter 7, p. 109). In addition, collection, elaboration, and interpretation of data should be part of a community development strategy ; that means, the monitoring itself should benefit from the direct involvement of the community: its members and leaders, local politicians and local experts. We know from various countries, that the local and community level is the level best fit for the direct and active participation of children and minors themselves. Therefore, children's experience should not be neglected as an indispensable resource in the monitoring process at community level.

Chapter 8 is dedicated to measuring and monitoring children's well-being and policy making. Again, a number of criteria are indicated for validating the relevance of indicators for children's well-being as well as their potential for influencing policy making processes. The chapter is based on the experience of five case studies on child poverty from Ireland, South-Africa, France, Israel and the U.S.A., which were carried out in the international project.

In my view, with child poverty, an excellent case in point was selected, because firstly, increasingly concerns are expressed about the levels of child poverty in most developed industrialised countries, and secondly, there is hardly any other phenomenon generating so many misunderstandings, as child poverty. While some think of child poverty in terms of the situation of children from poor communities or families, others connect it rather with an unfair intergenerational distribution of material resources in society. There cannot be any doubt that both phenomena need political attention and intervention, however, the political answers must be different. Therefore, researchers have to be lucid in presenting and interpreting the respective types and levels of child poverty, in order to facilitate the political debate.

The authors of the book as well as the participants in the project are aware that the results presented are not the final word; they are rather suggestions for further debate and elaboration. There can be no doubt that considerable progress has been made in this field throughout the last years, but much work remains to be done in the forthcoming years.

Helmut Wintersberger

Vienna

ACKNOWLEDGEMENTS

This book is an outcome of the work of many. It is the outcome of an extensive international collaboration through a 4 years international project. Although it is not an official summary, this book is a direct outcome of the project and would have not become a reality without it.

Special thanks are due to the project co-sponsors, who with almost no external support have funded the project, administrated it and brought it to its successful completion. We therefore express our deepest gratitude on behalf of all the project members and the authors of this book to: The Israeli National Council for the Child (NCC) who initiated the project and served as its secretariat and its coordinator. Special thanks are due to the NCC Executive Director Dr. Yitzhack Kadman who gave constant support to this work and to Ms. Elizabeth Levi and Ms. Galia Efrat who served as the project's administrative coordinators.

The J.D.C-Brookdale Institute was among the founders of the project and its director, Prof. Jack Habib as well as its faculty members Ms. Talal Dolev and Prof. Jona Rosenfeld have contributed a lot to our project.

The European Center for Social Welfare Policy and Research and especially Dr. Helmut Wintersberger, the former director of their childhood program, the third founder of the project. Dr. Wintersberger has played a crucial role in the development of the project as well as in bringing this book to publication. We would like to thank Helmut for his wisdom and helpful comments as well as for writing the preface for this book.

The International Youth Foundation under the leadership of its president Mr. Rick Little and the active engagement of Ms. Karen Pittman, Ms. Merita Irby and Dr. Herbert Friedman were active partners in this endeavour. We would especially like to thank Herb Friedman for his very useful comments on earlier versions of this book and for sharing his vast expertise with us.

The Institute for Families in Society at the University of South Carolina, under the leadership of its former director - Prof. Gary Melton has played a major role in our project. They have hosted our third meeting and supplied two of this book's co-authors. We would like also to thank Gary Melton and his colleagues at the Institute on Family and Neighborhood Life at Clemson University for their continuing support and express a personal gratitude to Gary for going over numerous drafts of this book and sharing his wisdom and knowledge so willingly. Both Childwatch International and the JDC-Israel, Children at Risk domain were important partners in this endeavor. Personal thanks are due to Dr. Per Miljeteig and Ms. Chana Katz. The University of Molise at Campobasso Italy and our dear friend Prof. Angelo Saporiti showed us all what hospitality is, and how substantial progress can be made while not neglecting the joy of life.

The National Center for Children in Poverty (NCCP) at Columbia University has also played a major role in our work and contributed yet another author of this book.

The Chapin Hall Center for Children at the University of Chicago is the last on our list of the project co-sponsors, but its contribution was certainly not the least. Apart from contributing two co-authors for this book, special thanks are due to Chapin Hall's communication department and especially to Ms. Anne Clary and Ms. Heather Hinko for the assistance in the final preparation of this volume.

But thanks are due not only to institutions; many have contributed to our book on the individual level. First and foremost are our colleagues and friends who participated in the International Project. Our work is based our joint work and the rich contribution of our friends. We would like to express special thanks to our friends and colleagues who went over the draft versions of this book and helped us do a better job. The list includes: Brett Brown, Talal Dolev, Herb Friedman, Frank Furstenberg, Don Hernandez, An-Magritt Jensen, Karen Kidder, Laura Lippman, Gary Melton, Alan Prout, Jens Qvortrup, Jona Rosenfeld, Judith Torney-Purta, and Helmut Wintersberger.

We would also like to express our thanks to the Kluwer Academic press, especially to Ms. Sabine Wesseldijk and her assistant Ms. Anny Burer as well as to Prof. Alex C. Michalos – the social indicators series editor, and the anonymous reviewers. They all made what often is a tiring and uncomfortable process of publishing a book into an enjoyable one.

Finnaly, the co-authors and members of the International Project are grateful for the leadership of Asher Ben-Arieh whose vision and commitment to our work made the project and this book a reality. And personal thanks from Asher to his colleagues at the NCC – for being a true supportive environment and to the Chapin Hall Center for Children for a wonderful fellowship year which without it would be hard to imagine the completion of this book.

INTRODUCTION

This project began during the fall of 1994. A small group of experts working on measuring and monitoring the state of children began to realize that they shared some common concerns. Not the least among them was the failure to measure the state of children beyond survival or their basic needs. This concern evolved into an international project, which in its turn led, among other things, to the publication of this volume.

Initiated by the Israeli National Council for the Child (NCC) and co-sponsored by a number of European, American., Israeli, and other international institutions, organisations, and foundations, a first-of-its- kind international workshop was convened in Jerusalem in January 1996. Its purpose was to re-examine existing measurements and indicators of children's well-being and to suggest new ones that illuminated more than survival rates and the attainment of basic needs. All the papers presented in this workshop were later published as a special Eurosocial Report (Ben-Arieh & Wintersberger, 1997), which offers the best description of the founding concepts of the international project.

The members of this international project, some eighty experts from twenty-seven countries, have reconvened twice since then--in Campobasso, Italy and South Carolina, United States. In those meetings as well as in between them the project members have identified the basic concepts and assumptions that should guide future work in this field. They identified five domains of children's well-being and some fifty indicators and measurements.

This book presents those discussions and agreements. It is not, however, a project summary. It is a joint effort of a small group of the project members to lay out our interpretation of the field of measuring and monitoring children's well-being, and to make the strongest possible case for continued and increased commitment to the development of meaningful indicators of the well-being of children and for monitoring the degree to which societies are able to use them to improve children's lives. Although we believe we managed to transfer accurately the project's spirit and conclusions, this volume is certainly our personal interpretation and therefore our sole responsibility.

Although we were heavily influenced by the project members and outcomes, we made a number of working decisions:

In the book, we refer to children without stating a specific age group. Children are defined as human beings between the ages of 0-18. We deliberately avoided any breakdown into specific age groups (such as adolescents or young children) because we believe that the concepts are the same for all children. Furthermore, children are defined legally in most of the world, as well as in the United Nations Convention on the Rights of the Child (CRC), as being between those ages. We argue that any effort to distinguish conceptually among children according to age groups would be wrong and could lead to negative results for the children themselves (for example, lowering the age of adulthood responsibility or suggesting that after a certain age children are unchangeable). We do, however, acknowledge the need for developing different measures to be used among different age groups. Furthermore, we believe that the age of the child should play a major role in analyzing the data collected.

Although our working group discussions were based on the contributions of experts from twenty-seven countries, the vast majority of the project members (as well as all the authors of this volume) are from industrialized countries dominated by western culture. Yet, most of the world's child population lives in developing countries, and thus is subject to different hazards and needs. Nevertheless, we believe that our efforts focused on children from industrialized countries—to define and recommend research for children's well-being beyond survival—is necessary and appropriate.

We also believe that all children of the world will benefit from this work and that they, too, deserve to share in our aspiration that their lives might reach beyond mere survival or access to basic services.

We have not shied away from making moral judgments. In fact, we openly embrace certain values as criteria for indicators or measurements of children's well-being. Naturally, the values we adopted are those that are accepted by our communities; they include the concepts of children's rights and democracy as important values that play a major role in defining children's well-being. We realize that children's well-being is heavily culture-contingent we stress that cultural context should be taken into account when analyzing the data and drawing implications for policies.

Finally, we stress throughout the book the need to make strong connections between the efforts to enrich our knowledge and policies on the one hand, and programs aimed at promoting children's well-being on the other. In other words, we emphasize our belief in *measuring for doing*. Although we do not underestimate the importance of knowledge per se for the human society, we argue in this book for the *application* of that knowledge for the improvement of children's everyday lives.

So this is how the project began and a little about what guided our work. It is time now to turn to where we hope this work will lead. We expect this volume to serve as a call to individuals, organizations, and governments to learn more about the state of their children. Chapter 1 lays out the rationale for such efforts. In Chapter 2, in order to strengthen our call, we present the progress and status of efforts similar to ours that have been carried out around the world. In a way we are saying, "Look, so many are already doing this work. You should be a part of this effort."

But as one might suspect, we are not willing to settle for just any kind of measuring and monitoring effort. Thus in Chapter 3 we present the basic assumptions and concepts that we came to use and that we suggest would be useful for projects around the world. In Chapter 4, we suggest five possible domains of children's well-being within the context of six questions we would like to have answered about our children's lives.

We then turn, in Chapter 5, to present forty-nine possible indicators and measurements of children's well-being. Although we avoid judging the relative importance of these indicators in comparison with others, we present strong arguments for the credibility of each.

Realizing the complexity of such a task, we present in Chapter 6 the various sources of information that could be used to collect data on children's lives and well-being. Finally, with respect to our commitment to measuring for doing, Chapters 7 and 8 are devoted to possible uses of these indicators to promote children's well-being through the policy- making process, in their communities, and more broadly in governmental and nongovernmental organizations.

This book will not provide all the answers; much work remains to be done, especially if we would like to have better knowledge of our children's lives as well as better strategies for using such knowledge to promote their well-being. Chapter 9 summarizes the major points of the book and lays out an agenda for the future--an agenda that will use the work on behalf of children's well-being as a starting point or benchmark on the long road towards improving the lives of all our children.

CHAPTER 1

THE RATIONALE FOR MEASURING AND MONITORING CHILDREN'S WELL-BEING

This volume is entirely devoted to the subject of measuring and monitoring children's[1] well-being. It is not intended primarily to be an academic or research venture, but rather to provide a tool for practitioners, professionals, and, in fact, anyone who works with and for children. We believe that such a tool is essential for any meaningful effort to promote the well-being of children. Initially, some four years ago, a small group of children's advocates--practitioners and researchers--asked themselves the following question: if measuring and monitoring children's well-being is so obviously important and has such positive potential, why do we still face numerous problems in developing and implementing the use of these valuable tools? Moreover, where such tools do exist, the practice of actual and consistent monitoring is rare.

In what has been called the Information Age, we know surprisingly little about the state of our children. Given the widely held assumption that information is a source of power, it is striking that this area of knowledge has not been more fully developed in order to gain power on behalf of children. The fact that we do not know, acquire, and use information about children's well-being raises the question of what, specifically, there is to gain from such an effort?

In order to answer that question, this chapter will deal with three major issues: the power of information, the reasons for measuring the well-being of children, and the possible benefits accruing from such an effort.

THE POWER OF INFORMATION

Information in general and data in particular have the power to shape and influence policies and services. A report by the American National Research Council to the U.S. Senate states that,

---

[1] Further to what was stated in the introduction it should be clear that we refer to the age group of 0-18 while using the term children.

A. Ben-Arieh et al (eds.), Measuring and Monitoring Children's Well-Being, 1–10.
© 2001 *Kluwer Academic Publishers. Printed in the Netherlands.*

> The essential demand for evaluating and analyzing
> alternative government plans, no matter what the
> nature and type of analysis or the tools and methods
> required, is that there is data to analyze. Good data is
> the critical component for any theoretical model or
> method of analysis aimed at producing good
> evaluations and policy analysis (as cited in Ben-
> Arieh, 1997 p. 29).

It is hard to disagree that knowledge and information have power, especially when thoughtful use is made of them. This power is held by those who manage, control access, and are aware of the options for its use. The controller of information may exercise power by using it or retaining it-- making decisions that are based on the data possessed or keeping it from others in order to limit criticism or to prevent others from using the information for their own purposes.

The claim that systematic collection and publication of information may threaten decision makers is not a new one. These activities shed light on the decisions taken and expose the decisions to public debate, thus preventing policy makers from concealing their decisions and actions behind a veil of ignorance. Well-conceived studies provide the public with an independent basis for evaluating policies and programs against stated goals and objectives.

But collecting data should not be considered only, or even primarily, as a threat. In most cases, data collection carries a promise. History has taught us that knowledge is more likely to produce better outcomes than ignorance. Knowledge provides a firm foundation for better decisions and more appropriate services and plans.

Some of the best examples of the power of information in promoting children's well-being can be drawn from the effort of UNICEF to measure the state of the world's children. Simply counting the number of lives taken by rubella led to a dramatic increase in immunization rates, which led in turn to a decrease in the number of children dying from the disease (Adamson & Morrison, 1995). In Israel, measuring the prevalence of drug-addicted newborns and monitoring the policies aimed at promoting their health led to new and better policies (Kadman & Gilat, 1994). In the face of such important outcomes, we argue that the development and dissemination of information relating to children's well-being outweighs any risk to individuals or the regimes they serve.

Building the power of any data or information is contingent on both demand and the ability to meet that demand. The American National Research Council report mentioned above states that,

> Since the establishment of the U.S. federal government in 1789, the decision makers at the legislative and executive level demanded data and information in order to decide between alternatives of public policy. Nevertheless, through most of this nation's history, the provision of data for policy purposes has been segmental and ad-hoc (as cited in Ben-Arieh, 1997 p. 30).

The lack of data on children's well-being is due, in part, to a lack of demand, the absence of any institutionalized means of collecting data on children, and the lack of agreed-upon indicators of well-being, which would permit consistent collection of data and comparisons over time and place.

To conclude, data and information can provide power to those who hold it. The way the holders of the information use it and the contexts in which they operate will shape the kind and scope of power they wield. In order to strengthen our power to understand and advance children's well-being, we must create systematic and institutionalized methods of collecting information and must secure access for child advocates to governmental and nongovernmental decision making.

WHY MEASURE CHILDREN'S WELL-BEING?

Any effort to answer this question requires a deeper look into three concepts. First, we should ask ourselves why we should measure *societal* well-being. Second, we should ask why we should measure *children's* well-being independently from the well-being of the whole society. Finally, we should deal with the level of analysis; in particular, we should consider the need for knowledge about children's well-being at the local, regional, national, and international levels and the potential usefulness of such knowledge at each level.

The Social Measurement Movement

Many factors influence and shape policies in general and social policies in particular. Over the last three decades, the importance attributed to knowledge, expertise, and information as factors that shape policies has been growing (Banting, 1979; Berger, 1980). In an era of rapid change and increasing sources of information, decision making has become more complex.   Decision makers seek, or are expected to seek, all relevant information before deciding between different alternatives and setting priorities, as well as when evaluating the effectiveness of any given policy (Brannen, 1986; Bulmer, 1986; Heller, 1986). In order to assist those making social policies, social scientists, especially since the early 1960s, have developed the tool of *social indicators*. Social indicators are

> quantitative data that serve as indexes to socially important conditions of the society (Biderman, 1966 p. 69).

In a sense, the social indicators represent yet another step in satisfying the basic human desire to develop new types of knowledge in order to know more about human society (Gross, 1966).   Much of the development of social indicators resulted from the efforts of policy makers in the U.S. to create a quantitative picture of the society in which they were living as well as of the changes this society was undergoing. Social indicators represent a wide range of data development and analysis, as well as conceptual and methodological efforts to measure and monitor various social dimensions. They are used to help define policy targets, monitor policy implementation, and evaluate policy influence. Social indicators can also be used to describe social processes and to contribute to public awareness of social problems and the need to address those problems (Miles, 1985).

Much of the enthusiasm and eagerness to develop and use social indicators can be attributed to the belief in their usefulness for planning and guiding social policies (Sheldon & Parke, 1975) as well as their relevance to building models for social services (Land, 1975). Today, the use of social indicators is widely accepted and recognized as an important tool in the making of social policies. Thus, there is no longer a question of the need for social indicators, but rather of the type and quality of those used. There is a need to be certain that the indicators are used and available, and are updated and adequate to the growing needs of policy makers.

Unfortunately, this is not the case in the area of children's policies. There is a basic lack of information on child-related indicators, and what exists is often outdated and inadequate. This situation is the outcome of the lack of demand and the failure to allocate adequate resources for this task.

Children as a Distinct Group

We have stated in the previous section that social indicators are used to measure and monitor changes in the status of individuals and societal well-being in various domains. Sub-fields of social indicators concentrating on those that monitor and measure the status and changes of individuals and population groups in specific domains and areas of life (i.e.,, health, public safety, education, employment, income, housing, leisure and recreation, and population) have begun to emerge.

Although there has been rapid development of health and education indicators (Bottani, 1994), there are almost no social indicators that concentrate on a specific culture or population group. Instead, we use the same social indicators in all cultures and population groups. Similarly, there has been little development of social indicators for different age groups. Only in the last 15 years, with the rise of gerontology as a profession, can we find development of indicators on the social status of the elderly.

Recently, we have also seen new attention to the development of indicators on the social status of children. Although UNICEF has been publishing its *State of the World's Children* reports for more than 20 years, significant growth in attention to child-oriented social indicators has become evident only recently (See Appendix 1 for numerous examples).

The development of child-oriented social indicators is still in its infancy. Those working in the field have had to cope with many question and doubts. Even the basic idea that children are a unique and separate population group requiring special policies is still controversial. It is particularly hard to convince skeptics that children deserve a separate policy that could and sometimes does differ from family policy (Qvortrup, 1994). One impetus for the development of special social indicators for children has been the recognition of children's rights and implementation obligations states have accepted under international law. These developments are discussed in Chapters 2 and 3.

Unfortunately, it is still the case that efforts to collect data specifically focused on children are frequently hampered by the argument that such efforts are unnecessary since children are already included in data collected about families and/or mothers. Jensen and Saporiti in 1992 completed a thorough study[2] of existing data in sixteen industrialized countries and concluded,

> ...that there was a dearth with respect to statistical
> data about children (Jensen & Saporiti, 1992 p. 9).

Several attempts to collect data on children led to a common conclusion that children were not sufficiently visible in the industrialized countries'

---

[2] This study was a part of the larger European project - described in detail in chapter 2.

systems of social accounting (Barnhorst & Johnson, 1991; Ben-Arieh, 1992-1995; Grant & Adamson, 1979-1995; Jensen & Saporiti, 1992).

Why? Otherwise, states would have to acknowledge that

> in order to make any particular population group
> visible the members of this group - in this case
> children - must be made the unit of observation
> (Jensen & Saporiti, 1992 p. 9).

Clearly, industrialized states have been unwilling to collect data in this manner.

Adamson argues that, while collecting data on economic trends and the social status of families and even the elderly is becoming second nature to those who make economic and social decisions, collecting data on children as a unique and special population group is far from standard (Adamson & Morrison, 1995).

It is our assumption that children are a unique and distinct population group who need and deserve a unique policy or set of policies to promote their well-being. The best interest of the child may not only differ from that of the family or parents, but may even conflict with it. In order to shape appropriate and effective policies for children, a flow of data and information regarding their status, as well as the changes they experience and are facing, is also required. An ongoing effort is necessary in order to develop appropriate children's social indicators and to measure their well-being if we seek to improve their well-being by implementing the policies and services they deserve.

Measuring the State of Children's Well-Being at Various Levels

Recent years have shown a growing interest in focusing on communities and neighborhoods as the context of children's well-being, and the need to focus policies and programs in these areas. There has been an accompanying increase of interest in the level at which data on children's well-being should be collected and in the necessity for such data in planning, policymaking, and evaluation. Any theoretical model or method of analysis, as with any policy, program, or service planning and evaluation, is contingent upon the availability of good data, regardless of the size or scale of the community under study.

It has become increasingly clear that collecting data and analyzing cannot be considered an exclusively national or governmental responsibility.

Around the world, we have seen a shift in the responsibility for our children's well-being from federal or national agencies to regional, district, municipal, or community- level agencies. In virtually all countries, it is evident that data on children's well-being is not yet available at these new levels and, therefore, new data will be needed.

To sum up, better understanding of the need for child-centered data at new levels of analysis is the first necessary step on the long road to developing and collecting such data. Better understanding of the benefits of such an effort is essential if we are to convince policy makers as well as scholars of the importance of this effort.

BENEFITS OF MEASURING AND MONITORING

An ongoing effort to measure and monitor children's well-being will enable societies to inform their policies, galvanize and reward effort, mark their achievements, introduce accountability, and be a means by which sustained pressure can be brought to bear for the fulfillment of political promises (Adamson & Morrison, 1995). Many benefits may be gained from measuring children's well-being. Only a few are cited here, and more will be discussed in the following chapters of this volume.

Enhancing Knowledge

Measuring children's well-being will provide new and important information which will enhance professional knowledge concerning childhood and children. Research has established that statistical information is one of the most cited forms of knowledge (Bulmer, 1986). Knowing the status of children will enable us to identify specific groups of children who are in distress or are disadvantaged relative to others, as well as those who are doing well.

Knowing the status of various groups of children is important for both policy planning and implementation. Knowing the status of disadvantaged groups will help in developing policies and ideas to promote their well-being, and knowing the status of those children who are doing well will enable us to enrich our knowledge regarding what works in giving children better lives.

Measuring children's well-being will enable us to know who our children are, as well as their economic and social situation, their health, and their perceptions and feelings about their current situation and future possibilities.

We might know how many of our children live in poor families, but we do not know the consequences of living in such conditions (Duncan & Brooks-Gunn, 1997).

Measuring the status of children will not only shed light on their well-being, but will also reveal how well or how poorly we are dealing with our obligations to our children. We should know, for example, how many of our children are able to enjoy recreational activities and whether their playgrounds are safe. We should have better knowledge for each country about the level and type of social investment in the young and the extent and degree of concern with particular areas of children's well-being and children's rights.

To conclude, data collected by measuring children's well-being, will give us the option to build a basis for discussion about needs, programs, priorities, and directions for the future.

Providing tools for better planning

Knowledge and information are the basics of any planning process. When accepting the need for planning services and policies for children, one must accept the need for knowledge. Such knowledge, when we are dealing with children, cannot be obtained without making children the focus for the collection of data and information. Measuring children's well-being will provide planners with new insights born of a new perspective on children's lives. This new perspective forces decision makers to view children very differently than when children are represented by adults. For example, acquiring accurate information about children's subjective perceptions of safety or of their leisure time activities cannot be gained by asking adults, but only by asking children themselves.

This effort will also help to illuminate the relative position of children in comparison to other age groups in society. In addition, it has the potential to clarify and dramatize children's contributions to society, thereby providing an "economic" rationale for investing more resources in children (Jensen & Saporiti, 1992; Wintersberger, 1997).

Knowing the status of children also means knowing the gaps in our knowledge about the problems and needs of children--both of the entire child population in a society and of specific groups within it. Any planning of services or policies for children will have to be informed by data about disadvantaged groups of children, and the gaps and deficiencies in the services and opportunities' for them. Knowing the status of children is essential to good planning and is the first step in planning services and policies that will be directed to the specific needs of specific groups of children. A good example of the potential for improving policies is that knowledge about the status of children in different geographical areas or from different population groups will enable planners to engage in differential resource allocation in order to address the problem and needs of each geographic area or population group.

Knowing more about children's well-being will also enable us to compare the status of children across different time periods and in different locations. Such comparisons are essential if we want to evaluate the policies that are under our control in order to discern whether they are helping children to do better or are contributing or failing to prevent negative consequences for children.

Making Monitoring Possible

Knowing the status of children and planning well-designed policies with clear strategies and objectives is not enough. Monitoring the implementation of policies and services is no less important. A constant process of measuring the status of children will serve as a vital tool for monitoring their well-being and the policies, services and programs aimed at improving their lives.

Measuring the status of children will provide a tool for the ongoing mission of improving children's well-being. When collected and reported regularly, the information will shed light on the extent to which policies are indeed improving the lives of children in society as a whole and among particular groups of children. Consistent and closer monitoring of social indicators of children's well-being will enable government, nongovernmental organizations, the media, and the public to observe achievements for children, as well as the rate of positive change. It will also help identify deficiencies and failures. Finally, it will make possible comparisons over time and space, within single countries, and also across countries.

The World Summit for Children recognized development of social indicators as a vital part of their plan for action.

> Each country should establish appropriate mechanisms for the regular and timely collection, analysis and publication of data required to monitor relevant social indicators relating to the well-being of children (Adamson & Morrison, 1993 p. 4).

Such measurement would become an important tool for monitoring and evaluating the success and failure of policies. It would enable us to analyze more precisely at all levels the consequences of any particular policies and would enable us to compare the situation of children in different places within and across societies. Doing so would make possible the necessary adjustments and changes each policy and plan need in order to remain relevant and adequate to the ever-changing needs of children.

Knowing for the sake of doing

Knowing for the sake of knowing, planning, and even monitoring is not enough. Measuring children's well-being should be undertaken for the sake of improving the status of children. The knowledge gained from such an effort should primarily be used for the sake of doing. The Israeli experience, as well as the Kids Count project in the United States and various other projects has shown that by regularly publishing a *State of the Child* report, one can attract public awareness that will lead to practical actions on behalf of children.

Perhaps, the best example of knowing the state of the children for the sake of doing is the ongoing monitoring effort done by UNICEF in the *State of the World's Children*. This effort, over the past 20 years, to collect and publish accurate information about the living conditions of children, has led to a series of practical steps carried out in developing countries. The results have been surprisingly good, with many countries doubling their immunization and school enrollment rates, and cutting by half their under-5 and infant mortality rates (Adamson & Morrison, 1995; Bellamy, 1996-1999; Grant & Adamson, 1979-1995).

It is now time to move forward and find the effective and appropriate indicators to measure children's well-being. Selecting accurate and useful indicators will enable us to measure the state of the child effectively, and means measuring for the sake of doing—to improve the lives of children. There can be no doubt that an effort to measure children's well-being will be beneficial when taken seriously by those who work and care for children.

CHAPTER 2

EXISTING EFFORTS AROUND THE WORLD

After dealing in the previous chapter with the rationale for measuring and monitoring children's well-being, in this chapter we explore the current efforts around the world. First, we describe the current field of indicators of children's well-being. Second, we identify central themes and topics from various existing reports. Third, we describe a number of existing efforts around the world, while differentiating among them according to format and content.

CURRENT FIELD OF CHILDREN'S WELL-BEING INDICATORS

Although there is a long history of sociological and demographic study of social trends using statistical indicators, it was the publication of Bauer's book entitled *Social Indicators* (Bauer, 1966) that prompted the widespread use of the term *social indicators*. One of the key objectives of the early social indicators effort was to assess the extent to which government programs or policies were achieving their stated objectives. In order to evaluate or monitor changes taking place in society, emphasis was placed on the utility of social indicators within social system models (Land, 1975).

Concerns about monitoring the situation of children are also not new. UNICEF has published its *State of the World's Children* report since 1979. This annual review of basic indicators of children's survival and development has helped create a global awareness of the need for monitoring how children fare. There have been various initiatives, such as the "European Childhood Project," to become more specific and accurate about describing the situation of children, in more detail and with quantitative data. And certainly there have been many local initiatives to address the issue of obtaining better and more reliable information on the actual situation of children and their well-being. These efforts have been initiated by researchers, public agencies and NGO's within their spheres of interest or operation (Miljeteig, 1997).

Over the past decade, there has been growing interest in measuring the well-being of children, due in part to a movement toward accountability-

11

A. Ben-Arieh et al (eds.), Measuring and Monitoring Children's Well-Being, 11–32.
© 2001 *Kluwer Academic Publishers. Printed in the Netherlands.*

based public policies that require increasing amounts of data to provide more accurate measures of the conditions children face and the outcomes various programs achieve. At the same time, rapid changes in family life also have prompted an increased demand from child development professionals, social scientists, and the public for a better picture of children's social well-being (Lee, 1997).

By identifying key indicators and their relationships to specific outcomes or social well-being measures, these modeling efforts placed emphasis not only on the descriptive function of social indicators but also on their analytic function. By and large, these functions were developed to provide better understanding of the impact of changes in children's policies and shifts in socio-demographic trends on the well-being of children (Zill, Sigal, & Brim, 1982). The recent growth of the childhood social indicators field can be seen in the publication of various state-of-the-child reports.[3] These reports have increased the level of interest in statistical descriptions of the well-being of children, thus resulting in several ongoing data reporting and compilation efforts in various countries (see Appendix 1 and following sections for examples).

Placing the Various Reports within a Framework

Numerous reports have recently been published on the state of children all over the world, especially in the last decade. Although many projects or studies of this kind have been launched in recent years, in this volume, we are concentrating on published reports only. We have made an extensive effort to analyze as many of these reports as possible, and the following sections are based on a review of more than 70 reports. (See Appendix 1 for the full list.) The reports can be put in the following framework, best described and understood in a matrix table.

Table 1. Types of State of the Child Reports

	The entire child population	A segment of the child population
Multi-issue reports		
Single-issue reports		
Integrated-issue reports		

---

[3] The term "state of the child report" is used here to describe any report dealing with the status of children at large and subgroups within the child population, regardless of the exact name of the report.

The *entire child population* means that the reports cover all the children at all ages from all population groups within a given geographical area. Those reports covering a *segment of the child population* describe only part of the child population identified by special need, special situation, age group, ethnic origin, or religion. *Single-issue reports* focus on only one aspect or domain of children's status, and *multi-issue reports* consist of a number of chapters, with each one devoted to a different domain or service system. *Integrated-issue reports* focus on one integrated index or cross-cutting issue.

It is worth stating however, that the suggested categories for organizing the various reports are not mutually exclusive. We have come across reports that are multi-issue but include a special chapter that is integrated. It is also evident that some overlap exists in the domains of children's well-being the various reports cover.

CENTRAL THEMES AND TOPICS OF EXISTING REPORTS

Based on our review of the state-of-the-child reports, we concluded that these reports are primarily organized by domains of children's lives, usually using domains defined by service systems.

In the following sections we first elaborate a little on the organizational aspects of the reports. Then, we explore the themes and domains that are covered in the various reports, regardless of their organizational framework.

Multi-Issue Reports on Children's Well-Being

As mentioned before, these reports consist of a number of chapters covering different domains of children's well-being. Reports in this category deal with at least two domains of children's well-being. A review of the existing reports shows that earlier reports have been more service oriented, usually organized according to the different social services they cover. The most common issues have been education, health, nutrition, day care, social services, housing, law and order, and probation. Many other multi-issue reports are organized according to criteria relevant to children, by means of the children themselves, their parents or the whole family's behavior or pattern of life. These reports include indicators on youth offenders, deviant behavior, sexual behavior, family formation, and family structure among others.

There are also reports organized around outcomes for children resulting from various causes. These include chapters on children who were victimized, either by neglect or abuse, or were victims of violence at school or in other settings. Other reports devote chapters to children living in poverty, to children living in war zones, and so on.

Although a number of other issues are covered by various reports, those mentioned above are the most common. In succeeding sections of this volume, we will discuss various other domains or issues covered in existing reports regardless of their organizational framework.

Single-Issue Reports on Children's Well-Being

Some reports are entirely focused on one specific issue or domain of children's well-being. These will naturally include various reports prepared and published by agencies that are concerned or have a mandate to provide a specific service for children. For example, the reports of the World Health Organization (WHO) provide information on child mortality rates or children's health. Similarly, various education ministries publish reports focusing on children's educational achievements and the police publish single-issue reports on juvenile offenders.

There are a growing number of attempts to develop single-issue reports on relatively new themes, such as the issue of children at risk (Children's Defense Fund, 1991-1999). Others concentrate on children who are neither working nor studying, teenage abortion, abuse and neglect cases, and calls to emergency hotlines by children.

Integrated-Issue Reports on Children's Well-Being

Recently, more reports have begun to incorporate integrated themes. Usually these reports present one comprehensive index for children's well-being. An early effort to provide an index of child welfare in Israel included housing density, education level of parents, and poverty (Habib, 1974).

Another report (Children's Defense Fund, 1991-1999) presents an index of risk based on the average number of a set of twenty at-risk indicators. The CDF index is similar to the Israeli list, but includes such additional items as smoking, vandalism, seat-belt non-use, and police contact.

Miringoff suggested an index for social health (Miringhoff & Opdycke, 1993; Miringoff, 1990), and has recently updated this suggested index

(Miringoff, Miringoff & Opdycke, 1999). UNICEF came forward in 1998 suggesting an index for children's well-being and research for several other indices are currently being developed at the National Center for Children in Poverty in New York (Bennett & Mosley, 1999).

Themes and Domains in Reports of Children's Well-Being

Beyond the traditional domains of children's well-being, which we discussed in the previous sections, some unique elements, in the form of nontraditional domains or special chapters, appear in various reports. In several reports, an explicit focus on children's rights has been added (Adamson & Morrison, 1995; Children's Defense Fund, 1991-1999; Shamgar-Handelman, 1990). Undoubtedly, the domain of children's rights is getting more attention and is more widely used, growing out of the universal acceptance and implementation of the U.N. Convention on the Rights of the Child (CRC).

Another domain is expenditure on children, whether private expenditure by families or public expenditure (Norwegian Commissioner for Children, 1990; Shamgar-Handelman, 1990) by program, or the total. A focus on access to basic sanitation (clean water, etc.) was featured in the UNICEF reports and in several other reports published mainly in nonindustrialized countries or by international organizations such as WHO.

Several reports include the domain of leisure/recreation and informal educational activities. The Israeli report, for example, devotes considerable attention to media, reading, cultural activities and opportunities, sports, enrichment courses, youth movements, and community centers (Ben-Arieh & Zionit, 1996-1999). The report of the Norwegian Commissioner for Children (1990) focuses specifically on organized recreational activities, while the U.S. Youth reports (Hobbs & Lippman, 1990) take a broader perspective, using the single category of "out-of-school experiences" to cover these activities.

Youth employment is another topic on which there is wide reporting; however, it is presented from a number of different perspectives. One perspective is that of youth who are at risk because they are not studying and not working (Ben-Arieh & Zionit, 1996-1999). Another perspective examines productive youth activities, which includes paid work, schoolwork, and housework (Jensen & Saporiti, 1992).

Another special domain addressed by several of the reports is that of the status of migrants, distinguishing between internal migrants and immigrants. Countries that have experienced or expect mass immigrations, not surprisingly, place more emphasis on immigrants (Ben-Arieh & Zionit, 1996-1999; Hernandez & Charney, 1998). Other reports highlight foreign children living in the country or children as migrants (Jensen & Saporiti, 1992; Norwegian Commissioner for Children, 1990), as do various publications of the ICDC in Florence. The latter basically provide comparable data on migrants or immigrants, but do not relate very much to concerns unique to migrants.

There are also reports that draw special attention to children in the judicial system. One analysis examines the various reasons for which children might have contact with the judicial system. Another, under the heading of alienation, includes various forms of deviance (Ben-Arieh & Zionit, 1996-1999; Testa & Lawlor, 1985).

In recent years, growing attention has been paid to the domain of the neighborhood or local communal environments. An example is the Illinois report (Testa & Lawlor, 1985), which includes data on such community facilities as libraries and playgrounds and residents' perception of the community. This domain is getting a lot of attention in various newly published or planned reports in the United States (Goerge & Lee, 2000).

Finally, a number of reports are focusing on the future by adding a separate chapter to a broad-perspective report or publishing a special report. One approach selects a number of indicators, which are believed to predict the future (Children's Defense Fund, 1991-1999). The other presents children's and youth's expectations for the future, as reflected in what they know about important social problems and the potential role those problems may play in their future (Norwegian Commissioner for Children, 1990).

EXISTING EFFORTS AND REPORTS

This section presents a partial list of various efforts and publications that monitor and measure the state of children around the world. When possible, we added a short description of the length, goals, and mandate of each report. What follows is by no means a complete list. Rather it is a modest effort to share with the readers the joint knowledge of some eighty participants in the international project that was the foundation for this book.

International Efforts

International efforts include any report or project that presents data and monitors the state of children in two or more countries. We begin with the work of UNICEF, not only because of its lead position, but mainly because of its major contribution to the field. Next, we describe some efforts by other international organizations, either governmental ones--such as the World Health Organization (WHO), the International Labor Organization (ILO), and UNESCO--or nongovernmental organizations, such as Childwatch International.

We go on to describe international projects, which although not designed to collect or analyze data, do promote new ways of thinking about measuring and monitoring the status of children. We also describe some international studies, which--although they do not focus primarily on children's well-being, nevertheless have made a significant contribution to the field.

UNICEF

Each year since 1979, UNICEF's *The State of the World's Children* presents the status of children as measured by a consistent set of variables. Furthermore, each year the report closely examines one key issue affecting children. The issues range from health, education, and nutrition to child labor and the impact of armed conflict on children. Since 1993, UNICEF has also published *The Progress of Nations*, which is designed to play a central role in monitoring global progress towards a set of goals for children's well-being that were established at the World Summit in 1990. In this new and innovative report, the nations of the world are ranked according to their achievements in child health, nutrition, education, family planning, and progress for women. The report also indicates setbacks. *The Progress of Nations* not only provides new and valuable data on vital issues affecting children, but it also helps governments, international organizations and nongovernmental organizations focus their priorities more effectively towards attaining the World Summit goals and securing the rights of all children. *The Progress of Nations* seeks to put an end to any severe inequalities or failure by states to advance the Summit goals by exposing such states to the conscience of the world community.

UNICEF's International Child Development Center (ICDC) has also played a major role in monitoring the state of children's well-being.. The ICDC *Regional Monitoring Report (MONEE)* project, started in 1992, has been concerned with monitoring the effects on children's well-being of public policies and social conditions in the countries in transition in Central and Eastern Europe, the Commonwealth of Independent States, and the Baltic States. The main goal has been to help ensure that public debate of social and resource distribution issues in the transition, which are of vital importance to children, are not overlooked. Its aim has been to help the formulation of better policies by, in particular, exploiting underused data already collected by local statistical agencies. The data has been assembled in Florence and used to produce an annual Regional Monitoring Report and other associated publications.

The ICDC is also heavily involved in a number of projects on child labor and children in poverty (especially in industrialized countries). Recently, ICDC has also started a project on children's well-being in Europe (Micklewright & Stewart, 1999). These projects may become very useful ongoing measuring and monitoring efforts.

Other International Agencies and Organizations
It is only natural that other international agencies and organizations were and are involved in efforts to measure and monitor children's well-being. Most of these are single-issue efforts focused on the specific interest of the organization. The World Health Organization (WHO), which includes as members almost every country in the world, has been working in its member states on child health--especially in developing countries--virtually from its inception more than 50 years ago. Over the past 25 years, WHO has been paying attention to adolescent health in these countries as well. This monitoring is especially important due to the broad reach of the organization.

WHO has produced hundreds of documents and many major publications on these subjects at global, regional, and national levels. Many of the early documents focused on the measurement of mortality and morbidity in children. The adolescent data ranges more widely and is beginning to touch on developmental issues, although there still is no comprehensive monitoring. Even if the positive emphasis on health and development is still relatively small, the trend is important to both policies and programming. The attempt to identify and broaden positive indicators and their measurement in children and adolescents certainly complements the work of WHO.

Another international organization involved in the field is the non-governmental research network, Childwatch International, which is dedicated to the promotion of children's rights and the Convention on the Rights of the Child (CRC) around the world. Funded primarily by the Norwegian government, Childwatch supports collaborative research aimed at producing the kind of information that would be useful in promoting public policies for identifying and developing indicators for implementation by the CRC. The Childwatch International *Indicators for Children's Rights*

Project is an international research project with the goal of use in monitoring the implementation of the Convention on the Rights of the Child. One major project has been the production of country case studies in Senegal, Nicaragua, Vietnam, Thailand, and Zimbabwe.

Since 1988, the Organization for Economic Development (OECD) has been developing an education indicator reporting system. The goal of the Indicators of Education Systems Project (INES) is to improve the comparability of education data across the OECD countries and to develop, collect, and report the condition of education in these countries while using a key set of indicators. The INES set of indicators includes measures of the demographic, social, and economic context of education; financial and human resources invested in education; access to education; participation and progress; the transition from school to work; the learning environment and organization of schools; student achievement; and the social and labor-market outcomes of education.

This OECD work has resulted in a series of reports published since 1992. *Education at a Glance: OECD Indicators, 1998* published by the Centre for Educational Research and Innovation, Indicators of Education Systems, Organization for Economic Co-operation and Development in 1998 was the last one to be published; another report is due in Spring 2000. The project was made possible by the financial and material support of the three countries responsible for coordinating the INES Network--the Netherlands, Sweden, and the U.S. In addition, work on the publication has been aided by a grant from the U.S. National Center for Education Statistics.

In addition, non-OECD member countries participate in the World Education Indicators (WEI) program, which OECD coordinates in cooperation with UNESCO. It is funded by the World Bank and facilitated by support from many OECD countries, notably Canada, the Netherlands, and the U.S. With inclusion of these countries, the coverage of *Education at a Glance* is extended to two-thirds of the world population. The countries participating in WEI are: Argentina, Brazil, Chile, China, India, Indonesia, Jordan, Malaysia, Paraguay, the Philippines, the Russian Federation, Uruguay, and Thailand. Israel has observer status in OECD's activities on education and has contributed to the OECD indicators on educational finance; their data are presented with the WEI participants.

International Projects
The projects described in this section were not primarily designed to conduct a study or collect data, but rather to promote new ways of thinking and to

invent new ways and new tools to advance the measuring and monitoring process.

Toward the end of the 1980s, an innovative international project was launched--the *Childhood as a Sociological Phenomena* project. This large international project was conducted under the auspices of the European Center for Social Welfare Policy and Research in Vienna. Its main objective was the establishment of foundations for a sub-field of sociology--childhood studies. The scholars involved wanted to collect and interpret relevant information about childhood and children from a sociological perspective. They convened for the first time in 1987 in Norway and officially closed at a conference in Denmark in 1992. Originally, scholars from nineteen countries participated, and by the concluding session, sixteen were still represented: Canada, Czechoslovakia, Denmark, England and Wales, Finland, Greece, Ireland, Israel, Italy, Norway, Scotland, Sweden, Switzerland, USA, and West Germany.

The project's main theoretical orientation was not the concept of the "child" in a developmental sense, but rather that of *childhood* as a social category. Childhood was not looked upon as a transient phase in an individual life, but was seen rather as a permanent structural segment of society. Childhood was placed in a relational or generational perspective, with its major group of reference being "adulthood" or "old age". On the whole, the project defined childhood as an integral part of the social system, and the social division of labor (as opposed to to seeing the developing child as an individual to be integrated into society).

The research project accomplished its major objectives: 1) available information on childhood in developed industrialized countries was collected and compiled; 2) areas insufficiently covered by research or statistics were identified; and 3) the adult-centric bias, generally prevailing in research and practice, was critiqued. From the data collected on the development of children's living conditions, the project group concluded that children had not benefited from the social and economic progress of recent decades. The shifts in the intergenerational division of resources has favored the adult and the elderly population instead.

The experience of the project underscored the importance of having a child focus, whether in research or in policies, as well as a need for establishing children's or childhood policies. The project resulted in the publication of a series of national reports, the Eurosocial Report Series 36/1990-1994: *Childhood as a Social Phenomenon*, was published. From the point of view of measuring the state of children, specific mention should be made of volume 36.17/1992 edited by A.M. Jensen & A. Saporiti entitled *Do Children Count? A Statistical Compendium.*

The project also generated a book published in 1994-- *Childhood Matters: Social Theory, Practice and Politics*-- as well as a number of conference papers. This innovative project has led (directly or indirectly) to the establishment of a number of new research committees on the sociology of children or childhood, as well as to the initiation of follow-up projects at the national and international levels. One of the results of this project, as well as of other efforts both internationally and nationally around the world, was the international project *Monitoring and Measuring Children's Well-being* from which this volume stems.

At the end of 1994, The National Council for the Child (NCC) in Israel initiated a new international endeavor. Discussions with a group of researchers from Europe, the USA, and Israel led to consensus regarding the need for new and creative methods for measuring the status of children. It was agreed that the group would focus on the development of measures for aspects of children's lives beyond survival. These discussions led to the first international workshop "Measuring and Monitoring the State of Children - Beyond Survival" that was held in January 1996 in Jerusalem. This international gathering of thirty-five experts from twenty countries later developed into a 3-year international project.

The project participants included eighty experts from a variety of disciplines (social work, sociology, pediatrics, psychology, law, statistics, economics, and more) from twenty-eight countries. Participants came from NGOs, universities, research centers, bureaus of census, government ministries and institutions, and international organizations and foundations. Project participants met three times, every eighteen months, beginning in Jerusalem, Israel, then in Campobasso, Italy, and concluding in Charleston, South Carolina, United States. Between meetings, the participants worked in six working groups that prepared for the meetings and reported to the whole group.

The goals of the project were threefold:
1. To reexamine "old" measurements and indicators of children's well-being and compose a new set that would do the following: use the child as a unit of observation, accept the concepts of children's rights and childhood as a stage in itself, be based on a variety of sources of information, include positive indicators, and be policy oriented;
2. To suggest and invent ways and methods to use children's well-being indicators to promote the well-being of children;

3. To prepare a work plan for disseminating the work and using it for conducting international comparative research on the well-being of children.

Following the three international meetings and the work carried out in the six working groups between meetings, the following results were achieved. All twenty-five papers presented at the first meeting in Jerusalem were published in a special Eurosocial Report (No. 62). This volume of papers presents the rationale and basis of the project A list of guidelines on how to compose and use children's well-being indicators was agreed upon. This list was drawn from five case studies on the use of indicators to influence policies (from France, Israel, Ireland, South Africa, and the USA) and from the discussions that were held in one of the working groups and in the three plenary workshops.

The group decided to avoid the minefield of suggesting a single theoretical framework for children's well-being. The strong desire for more practical work, as well as the understanding that the theoretical definition of children's well-being is heavily culturally contingent, was the basis for that decision. The strategy the project adopted was to continue with a modified set of the five domains of children's well-being with which the group had become familiar. A clear understanding was reached that the categorization was not definitive, and that for some purposes the selected categories might not be the only important ones. The five domains were, however, defined and their theoretical basis elaborated by the working groups and, then, by the whole group. The domains chosen were the following: economic resources and contribution, personal life skills, civic life skills, safety, and children's activities. An effort has been made to construct these five domains within a flexible conceptual framework in order to better explain and highlight them and in order to explicate the indicators we chose for measuring and monitoring children's well-being.

A list of fifty indicators in all five domains was agreed upon. All the indicators were congruent with the principles and guidelines for indicators that the project participants had agreed upon, and all were theoretically based. A description of how the indicator might be measured and what data sources already exist accompanies each suggested indicator.

International studies (collecting data)
The *Luxembourg Income Study (LIS)* was launched in 1983 under the joint sponsorship of the government of Luxembourg and the Center for Population, Poverty and Policy Studies (CEPS) in Walferdange, Luxembourg. It is now funded on a continuing basis by the national science

and social science research foundations of its member countries and by some international funds.

The LIS Project has four goals:
1. To test the feasibility of creating a database consisting of social and economic household survey micro-data from different countries;
2. To provide a method of allowing researchers to access the data under privacy restrictions required by the countries providing the data;
3. To create a system that will allow research requests to be quickly processed and returned to users at remote locations; and
4. To promote comparative research on the economic and social status of populations in different countries.

Since its beginning, the experiment has grown into a cooperative research project that includes countries in Europe, North America, the Far East, and Australia. The database now contains information for more than twenty-five countries for one or more years. Negotiations are underway to add data from additional countries, including Korea, Mexico, and South Africa. In recent years, LIS is showing more and more interest in issues of child poverty, and its database makes feasible the measuring and monitoring of various dimensions of child poverty.

The *Health Behavior in School-Aged Children (HBSC)* is another cross-national study conducted in collaboration with the European Regional Office of the World Health Organization (WHO). It was initiated in 1983 by researchers from three countries--Finland, England, and Norway-- and since then has grown to thirty member countries (Currie, 1999). The HBSC aims to increase our understanding of health behaviors, health and well-being, and the social context of young people in the early adolescent years (11-15). A key objective is to use the research findings to inform and influence health policy, and, in particular, health promotion and health education policy, programs, and practice aimed at school-aged children at both national and international levels (Currie, 1999).

The first survey, conducted in 1983-84, was carried out in Austria, England, Finland and Norway, and since 1985-86 surveys have been conducted at 4-year intervals in a growing number of member countries. Twenty-eight countries participated in the 1997-98 survey--Austria, Flemish and French speaking Belgium, Canada, Czech Republic, Denmark, England, Estonia, Finland, France, Germany, Greece, Greenland, Hungary, Israel, Latvia, Lithuania, Northern Ireland, Norway, Poland, Portugal, Republic of Ireland, Russia, Scotland, Slovak Republic, Sweden, Switzerland, USA, and Wales.

The *Program for Indicators of Student Achieve*ment (PISA) is a study that grew out of the INES project (see details in the International Organizations section above). PISA responds to the need for regular assessments of student achievement among OECD countries. Beginning in 2000, achievement among 15-year-olds will be assessed in reading, mathematics, and science. Each cycle will focus on one subject area, beginning with reading in 2000.

The *Third International Mathematics and Science Study-Rep*eat (TIMSS-R) is another important study. During the 1998-99 school year, TIMSS was administered, at the eighth-grade level only, in forty countries and about fourteen states and localities in the U.S.   Most countries participating also participated in the initial TIMSS assessment in 1994-95, which assessed fourth-grade students and those at the end of secondary school.   Detailed contextual questions as well as classroom videotaping accompanied the testing of mathematics and science knowledge in the repeat study and will undoubtedly contribute a great deal to our knowledge about children's well-being.

Other international studies, which can be of great value to any effort to measure and monitor the well-being of children include the International Education Association Civic Education Study (CES), the Reading Literacy Study, and the International Social Survey Program (ISSP). Naturally there are many more international studies that have either direct or indirect interest in children's well-being. Unfortunately it is beyond the scope of this publication to name or describe them all.

National-Level Efforts

As mentioned above, we have decided to describe various attempts to measure and monitor the state of children at the national level. We have focussed on the following: efforts carried out by an official government or statutory institute; efforts carried out by academic groups; and efforts carried out by private foundations or NGOs. These distinctions are not only organizational; we found that the differentiation is reflected in the types of reports and the target audiences.

Government or Statutory Institutes
It seems that the question of how governments monitor the well-being of children is at least partly determined by the context and the institutional framework governments use to work with and on behalf of children

(Bradshaw & Barnes, 1999). This is especially evident when one looks into the impact of the universal ratification of the UN Convention on the Rights of the Child (CRC), which led to a legal obligation on the part of the ratifying countries to monitor and report on its implementation. Countries that have ratified the CRC are required to report to the ten-member Committee on the Rights of the Child within a 2-year period on the steps being taken to put the CRC into practice, with further reports due at 5-year intervals (Hodgkin & Newell, 1998).

Such reports, which are multiple-issue reports, quite naturally include special emphasis on the status of children's rights as well as their overall status and well-being. Although not all countries fulfill this obligation, a growing number of reports are being submitted to and reviewed by the CRC committee. Over time, these reports may play a role in monitoring efforts.

The rapid spread of the notion of children's rights has also led to the establishment of an Ombudsman, a Special Commissioner, and special departments or ministries for children's rights and/or children's well-being in a number of countries. These institutions, as a part of their work, publish special reports on the status of children (see, for example, Norwegian Commissioner for Children, 1990). Sometimes the reports focus on the overall status of children and are multi-issue; others are special reports on a single issue.

Similarly, the World Summit for Children and the goals agreed upon there have led to a number of government efforts to monitor achievements and progress toward the goals established there. In Mexico, for example, whose most recent report was published in 1999, an evaluation is prepared through an inter-ministerial committee consisting of the Secretary of Health, the Secretary of Public Education, the National Commission of Water and the National System for Integral Development of the Family.

The government departments devoted to children's concerns vary. In Greece, for example, children are the responsibility of the Ministry of Health and Welfare, in Italy the Ministry of Social Affairs, and in Germany and Austria the Ministry for the Family. However, in most countries, there is no single government department responsible for children and their well-being. Rather, their interests are divided among a range of ministries. A drawback of this institutional strategy is that children may become invisible in official statistics and reports. Some countries, such as Denmark, make children's interests integral to the work of all government departments rather than creating a separate ministry, which might neglect the issues of children's rights and well-being. (Bradshaw & Barnes, 1999).

More and more countries are taking steps to improve the level of coordination between government departments and the monitoring of children's well-being using the reporting requirements of the UN Convention on the Rights of the Child as justification. To prepare such reports, and to improve coordination, Belgium and Portugal each established a Commission on Children's Rights during 1996, and Italy established a National Observatory on Children's Problems and a parliamentary committee on children's problems in 1995. In Luxembourg, where an inter-ministerial group is responsible for the coordination of policies relating to children, an expert Committee 'Promoting the Rights of the Child' was established in 1993 (Bradshaw & Barnes, 1999).

An interesting example of such new governmental forums can be seen in the United States with the newly established *Federal Interagency Forum on Child and Family Statistics*. This forum started working in 1994, was formally extended through a Presidential Executive Order in 1997, and includes eighteen federal statistical agencies that collect data on children and their families. The heads of these agencies meet three to four times a year to plan and coordinate their activities to improve the efficiency and the utility of the federal statistical system in collecting data on children, youth, and their families, and to better serve the evolving needs of its constituency. The initial focus has been on the production and dissemination of social indicators, culminating in the production of an annual multi-issue report to the President entitled *America's Children: Key National Indicators of Well-being*. These reports (the first was published in 1997) contain roughly twenty-five key indicators of child and youth well-being in the areas of health, economic security, education, behavior, and social environment, in addition to several key demographic background measures.

A similar forum, *"The Inter-Ministerial Forum for Statistics on Children,"* was established in Israel during 1998, and in 1999 it produced a series of short reports entitled *Kids in Israel*. Similar forums have been working for some time in Norway and other Scandinavian countries.

Government work on this subject is far more extensive than establishing new forums or statutory institutes focusing on children's rights and well-being. It is evident that a growing number of government institutes as well as other statutory and formal institutes have been involved in recent years in efforts to measure and monitor the state of children. Their reports are usually multi-issue and service oriented, divided into domains defined by services (i.e.,, education, health, social services, and so on). Often, the reports are more traditional, focusing on survival issues, or rather on the absence of risk factors, and less on issues of child well-being.

Various government ministries are monitoring child well-being on a regular basis. One such effort is the *Trends in the Well-being of America's Children and Youth*. Carried out by Child Trends (and from now on by Westat Inc.) for the U.S. Department of Health and Human Services Assistant Secretary for Planning and Evaluation (DHHS/ASPE), this annual multi-issue report presents trend data on over ninety indicators of child and youth well-being (Child Trends, 1999).

The many reports on the well-being of children regularly produced by governments around the world vary greatly in their content. Maternal and child health statistics are published annually in Japan. Japan also publishes a multi-issue report on children's environment and a single-issue report on children under protection, every 5 years. Finland has a multi-issue annual statistical report on children that covers a range of indicators. In Belgium, annual reports on children in the Flemish and Walloon communities are published. Canada has published an annual report on children, based mainly on data from a longitudinal study, since 1996. Italy has also published an annual report on children since 1996. Norway annually publishes demographic statistics relating to children and their families, and statistics on children receiving social work assistance. In Germany, children's issues have until recently been included in the regular 5-year report on the family, although they have decided to move to biannual reports in the future (Bradshaw & Barnes, 1999).

An interesting multi-issue effort is being carried out by the National Center for Education Statistics at the U.S. Department of Education. This governmental center regularly publishes a report entitled *Youth Indicators: Trends in the Well-being of American Youth,* which provides national data on the well-being of youth in the areas of family, education, work, health, behavior, and attitudes. This report, first published in 1988, is updated every 2 to 3 years (Child Trends, 1999).

Many other reports have been published by governmental institutes on an ad hoc basis. Statistics New Zealand published a first-of-its-kind report on children in 1998, which provides details of household structure and economic circumstances, including housing tenure and parental labor force status. In terms of outcome measures, only a limited range of basic health and educational measures are reported. Similar reports are likely to be produced in the future (Bradshaw & Barnes, 1999).

In 1998, Finland produced a two-volume report on the well-being of children and young people, analyzing trends during the 1990s, and bringing together all known statistical information on children and young people. Other countries have also produced ad hoc statistical reports on children, which may or may not be repeated at a later date. These include the UK (1994), and Denmark (1995). Portugal has recently produced several new reports on children, covering child labor, children living in institutions, child abuse, and the results of a recent national survey of young people (Bradshaw & Barnes, 1999).

To sum up, it seems that national efforts to measure and monitor children's well-being are growing rapidly. The need for such reports is acknowledged; however, controversy remains over the format, categories, and scope of the reports.

Academic groups
Academic contributions to the area of measuring and monitoring child well-being is evident throughout the framing and conduct of almost all the reports. Academics have played a major role, from early efforts to define in a meaningful and useful way basic terms such as *welfare* and *well-being,* to their more recent contributions to the development of research and data collection tools. They have also contributed to the creation of innovative means of measuring the status of children in formulation of public policy recommendations for using newly acquired information to improve children's lives.

Academicians play a significant role in governmental as well as nongovernmental projects by serving on advisory committees, joining research teams, and conducting studies. Prominent examples include a number of the *Kids Count* state projects as well as a variety of other reports (see for example Barnhorst & Johnson, 1991). Usually such reports, prepared and published by academic institutes, are more oriented toward enriching our knowledge about child well-being than toward the direct steps of promoting children's well-being. Thus, such reports may measure the status of children and identify trends, but would not have as an objective the promotion of public policies to directly improve children's well-being.

We must also note the rapid development of child research centers around the world. Many of these centers are involved individually or with others in efforts to measure and monitor the well-being of children in their countries. Especially significant is the Norwegian Center for Child Research, which was probably the first. The European Center, Childhood Program has also made notable contributions with its sixteen country reports (an effort, described at length in the international section). Chapin Hall Center for Children at the University of Chicago published *State of the Child in Illinois* reports in 1980 and 1985 (with another that is forthcoming in 2000).

Private Foundations/NGOs
Various NGOs and private foundations play a critical role in measuring and monitoring children's well-being. Such groups usually produce reports that are advocacy oriented--intended as tools for working on behalf of children rather primarily as research. These groups often work directly or indirectly with academics, however, and their work is mutually reinforcing.

Most NGOs are less constrained by the various political requirements of governmental institutions. Many of the most innovative and imaginative reports have been developed by these organizations. Some of the earliest studies by these groups were especially successful in focusing on the child rather than on a social system. For example, in Austria, very useful annual reports on issues affecting children have been published by two large Catholic social welfare agencies lately (Bradshaw & Barnes, 1999).

Another example is *The State of America's Children*, an innovative and comprehensive guide to the well-being of children, produced by the Children's Defense Fund. This report has been published under several different titles since 1980 and has been produced every year but one. It contains analyses of issues relevant to the well-being of children and their families, and includes tables and charts that present both national trends and state-level data on children and their families. In recent years, the report also has included information on advocacy and program strategies that states and communities are using to safeguard children (Child Trends, 1999).

The State of the Child in Israel - A Statistical Abstract is another innovative example. Published every year since 1992 by the National Council for the Child, this report aims to place before the reader all the existing data on children in Israel. The report is unique in focusing on the child as a unit of observation, and in including data on various dimensions of children's lives, rather than being limited to those that endanger their development.

The Annie E. Casey Foundation *KIDS COUNT Project* is a national and state-by-state project to track the status of children in the United States. At the national level, the principal activity of the initiative is the publication of the annual *KIDS COUNT Data Book*, which includes measures of child and family well-being comparable across the fifty states. The national project, formally initiated in 1989, is intended to provide an accurate portrait of child well-being with comparable data at the state level, and to provide background data for all states. The goal of the *KIDS COUNT* project is to raise public awareness and to promote accountability. The first *KIDS COUNT Data Book: State Profiles of Child Well-being*, was released in

1990. The 1999 *KIDS COUNT Data book,* included profiles for the nation, and all fifty states, covered ten areas of well-being as well as expanded background data covering demographics, social and economic characteristics, child health insurance and child-care information, summary tables, introductory text, and additional materials. Additional publications have been produced by the project that provide state-level profiles of minority populations, based on data from the 1990 national census, and city-level profiles for primary child well-being indicators.

The Annie E. Casey Foundation also funds a network of state-level *KIDS COUNT* projects that provide detailed state, regional, and community-level views of the condition of children and families. The first seven *KIDS COUNT* state projects were funded in 1991. There are currently fifty local projects, in forty-nine states and the District of Columbia. Each state project annually publishes a data book, which presents child and family well-being indicators. Although each state project decides which indicators to include, and the format in which to present the information, many states base their data books quite closely on the national annual report, presenting the same indicators for the counties of the state. These data books often contain data that are valid and useful within individual states but are not available at the national level or are not comparable among states. Some states assemble data for their largest cities, regions, and other geographic areas (Child Trends, 1999).

In 1989, the Canadian Institute for Children's Health (CICH) published the first edition of *The Health of Canada's Children: A CICH Profile*. This statistical publication presented the first comprehensive picture of the state of child health in Canada. Five years later, CICH realized it was critical to reexamine children's health, and presented an updated picture of what had originally been found. *The Health of Canada's Children: A CICH Profile, 2nd Edition* highlights vast improvements in children's health and reveals emerging problems and issues. A third edition is due to be published.

Community-Level Efforts

In recent years, a new trend has emerged in the monitoring and measuring of children's well-being-- a focus on a specific community or region within a country. Reports are either published by community organizations or by national or other institutes. Some of the organizations use a similar framework to that of the national reports; some are unique and develop their own areas of interest and their own framework.

In some countries (including Spain, Austria, the Netherlands and Sweden), responsibility for children lies mainly at a regional or state level. In some cases, this allocation of responsibility gives rise to concerns about coordination: in Spain, for example, this concern was the main impetus for the creation in 1989 of an Inter-Ministerial Committee on Childhood and Youth. In Austria, each province has a Child and Youth Commissioner, and they meet regularly to form a permanent conference. In the Netherlands, responsibility for children has increasingly devolved to local and regional government in the belief that local control will strengthen accountability and responsiveness to needs. Similar examples are described in the *State of the Child in Jerusalem*, published by the National Council for the child in Israel and the Municipality of Jerusalem, and in the *Pathways for Healthier Communities Project* in Colorado.

CONCLUSIONS

Measuring and monitoring children's well-being is not an easy task, although it need not be more difficult or expensive than the measurement of other economic or social populations. In fact, as we have tried to show in this chapter, the task is already being carried out in various countries and settings by a variety of actors. Successful measuring and monitoring of child well-being requires a defined purpose. Why are we undertaking the project and for what audience? Whom are we trying to educate, inform, and persuade? As we have seen, different efforts have different purposes, which clearly shape their studies and reports.

We believe that the information gained from any effort to measure and monitor the well-being of children should increase the knowledge base in a way that enables us to identify specific groups of children--those who are in distress as well as those who are better off. Such an effort should provide tools for better planning. Measuring the state of children is the first step in planning services, programs, and policies that will better address the specific needs of different groups of children. It may provide planners with a view of children's living conditions different from that of adults. It may illuminate the relative position and needs of children in comparison to other age groups in society; and, by highlighting children's contributions, it may provide an "economic" rationale for investing more resources in children.

Regular measurement and publication of data on the state of children is vital for monitoring children's well-being and for monitoring and evaluating the success and failure of policies, services, and programs that seek to improve children's lives. Finally, reliable measurement of children's well-being could enable us to set goals for any social intervention on behalf of children and to evaluate the program's outcomes and achievements.

The only acceptable goal is improving children's well-being. Measuring and monitoring are not an end in themselves, but the means of providing a firm reliable basis for the more vital goal which is taking action to improve children's lives.

CHAPTER 3

UNDERLYING ASSUMPTIONS AND BASIC GUIDELINES FOR MEASURING AND MONITORING CHILDREN'S WELL-BEING

We began this volume by laying out our rationale for supporting efforts aimed at measuring and monitoring the well-being of children. We have also reviewed the efforts to date, addressing a wide variety of studies and reports, nationally and internationally, which reflect the very extensive agreement among governmental and nongovernmental organizations, scholars, and practitioners on the need to continue, and indeed to expand, these measuring and monitoring efforts. In this chapter, we provide an explanation of our basic assumptions, and explicate the general principles that have guided our research and recommendations.

We begin by considering our philosophy, which incorporates the assumption that children are the holders of basic human rights and that childhood is legitimately and properly viewed as a life stage in itself.

CHILDREN'S RIGHTS AS HUMAN RIGHTS

This notion has grown out of an international movement that starts from the belief that children are human beings and are entitled to treatment that respects their basic human dignity. This belief has, in the twentieth century, become so widespread that it is sometimes difficult to remember that not so long ago children were viewed as property, completely at the disposal of the adults in their lives. Although we have much left to do, we have come a long way in children's advocacy by establishing that children, as a group, while not little adults, are now, like other previously powerless groups, legitimate holders of rights.

Throughout the twentieth century, international law has reflected a growing consensus on the extension of basic human rights, both the extent of what constitutes rights and which groups are viewed as holders of these rights. Until the Charter and Judgment at Nuremberg following the Second World War, many nations had been unwilling to accept the idea that there were limits on the domestic exercise of their sovereign powers over their

33

A. Ben-Arieh et al (eds.), Measuring and Monitoring Children's Well-Being, 33–46.
© 2001 *Kluwer Academic Publishers. Printed in the Netherlands.*

own people. The atrocities of the Third Reich, however, so astounded observers with the realization of what a government could do to its own citizens that the international community denounced these acts as transgressions beyond any appropriate internal exercise of authority, and laid the groundwork for all subsequent international human rights agreements.

The first major evidence of this new international approach to human rights was the United Nations resolution referred to as the Universal Declaration of Human Rights. This document included two different sets of rights--civil and political rights, which were strongly advocated by the West, and economic, social, and cultural rights, which were championed by the Soviet Union and its allies. After over 20 years of drafting, the Declaration was transformed into two separate treaties, to address the political divisions over these rights[4]. In spite of continuing disagreement across nations about which groups are entitled to which rights, the international community has adopted a broad range of human rights treaties. In spite of differences in culture, religion, ethnicity, nationalism, ideology, race, language, and economic development, states have agreed on fundamental principles and guidelines for the treatment of those subject to their sovereignty.

Regional treaties focused, even more specifically, on their own regional approaches to human rights[5]. These conventions also set up monitoring systems either to allow complaints, including the creation of human rights courts, or to provide reports on the progress of implementation. States have also adopted numerous particular human rights treaties on a variety of subjects, such as racial discrimination, the rights of minorities, and the rights of women among others.

Children became the focus of the international development of human rights standards when, in 1989, following important declarations on the rights of children and many years of careful drafting and negotiation, the Convention on the Rights of the Child (CRC) was adopted by the United Nations. Unlike the Covenants mentioned above, the CRC incorporates a full range of rights for children. Furthermore, it integrates these rights and makes it clear that civil and political rights are indeed interdependent with economic, social, and cultural rights.

---

[4] The Covenant on Civil and Political Rights and the Covenant on Economic, Social and Cultural Rights 1966

[5] The European Convention for the Protection of Human Rights and Fundamental Freedoms, The African Charter on Human and Peoples Rights, and the American Convention on Human Rights all establish rights of protection from excessive state power as well as responsibilities for implementing human rights.

The Convention provides a very useful framework for monitoring children's rights and well-being. First, the convention has been ratified by 191 countries; only the United States and Somalia have not ratified, and the United States has signed. In fact, even without these ratifications, the treaty can be considered universally binding[6].

Second, the convention is comprehensive, as already indicated, covering a full set of interdependent rights. The clear underlying principle of human rights law, the dignity of the individual, is apparent throughout the treaty. All children are included,

> irrespective of the child's or his or her parent's or legal guardian's race, color, sex, language, religion, political or other opinion, national, ethnic or social origin, property, disability, birth or other status (Article 2).

Third, the CRC, in Part II, establishes a system of implementation. A Committee on the Rights of the Child, composed of ten experts selected so as to reflect geographic regions and principal legal systems (Article 43), is established to oversee implementation. States are required to submit reports periodically

> on the measures they have adopted which give effect to the rights...and on the progress made on the enjoyment of those rights... (Article 44, paragraph 1).

The Committee receives, reviews, and questions these reports, sometimes requesting further information, and normally suggesting further areas of needed implementation, providing detailed commentary and indicating concerns about omissions and needed future activity to move towards fulfilling the treaty obligations.

States are obligated to make their reports widely available to the public in their own countries, and they also accept the obligation to educate children and adults in their countries about the rights of the child. Groups beyond the government are invited to participate in the monitoring process; UNICEF and other UN agencies are

> entitled to be represented at the consideration of the implementation of such provisions...as fall within the scope of their mandate (Article 45).

---

[6] For the basis for arguing the binding nature of the convention see (Melton & Kaufman, 1997 p. 81-82)

The Committee may also transmit its reports to other organs of the UN and may request information or technical assistance from other UN organs, including from the General Assembly and the Office of the Secretary-General.

Fourth, the existence of the CRC has focused attention on the cross-national nature of many problems facing children, and also puts in place methods of international cooperation to address them. The preamble refers to

> the importance of international cooperation for improving the living conditions of children,

and Article 4 requires states to undertake measures to implement the convention

> to the maximum extent of their available resources and, where needed, within the framework of international cooperation.

Other articles make special mention of the needs of developing countries, calling on states to promote international cooperation to address problem areas (Articles 23, 24) or suggesting new international agreements where needed (Articles 11, 22).

Fifth, the convention is written in constitutional language--that is, language that is expansive and broad, requiring discussion and interpretation. It applies to developed and developing countries alike. The convention also is clear that the guiding principle of interpretation is the child's own experience. For civil and political rights, for example, the treaty enunciates that the rights of the child accused of violating the penal law is

> to be treated in a manner consistent with the child's sense of dignity and worth (Article 40.1).

This provision, then, gives a definition of the right and also a standard for how the right is to be implemented. The same is true in the realm of economic and social rights; for example, the treaty provides that a child's education should be directed towards

> the development of the child's personality, talents and mental and physical ability to their fullest potential (Article 29.1 (a)).

Thus, the convention clearly provides an integrated approach to interpretation, focusing on the idea that rights are an extension of personhood and personality. One guideline for monitoring children's rights and well-being, then, provided by the convention is establishing what it would take for children to *feel* that they are being treated with dignity. Proper monitoring would require a policy framework capable of producing strategies that would meet this objective.

The almost-universal ratification of the CRC, the breadth of the rights included, the constitutional nature of its language, the global approach to the issues, and the implementation provisions mean that the treaty offers a valuable framework for evaluating the indicators that we select and the monitoring process itself.

CHILDHOOD AS A STAGE IN ITSELF

Just as the CRC places children at the center of the human rights agenda, one of the most important dimensions of our work has been the central position of children in our deliberations and discussions about measuring and monitoring their well-being. Although it is possible and reasonable to develop indicators of child well-being by focusing on the outcomes of childhood, such indicators fail to consider the life stage of childhood, a stage that has its own sociological characteristics. Much of the literature on children, in fact, focuses on them exclusively as "future adults" or the members of the "next generation." Looking to the future is a legitimate and necessary activity, but we are committed to the inclusion of a child's perspective, one that would also accept the legitimate consideration of childhood as a stage in itself.

Thus, we focus, in large measure, on the activities and experiences of children while they are children, and on the construction of a clear picture of childhood and how childhood is experienced. This perspective is relatively new and not easily adopted, since we have all been socialized into certain ideas about children, ideas that are reinforced everywhere in society, and that emphasize children as potential, rather than actual members of society.

When viewing childhood as a stage in itself, we accept the idea that, although societal forces affect all members of the society, they are likely to affect children and adults quite differently. The elderly and the very young will disproportionately use the health care system, for example. Moreover, if we try to interpret the impact of societal change, the effects of industrialization or urbanization on the experience of being a child is very different from the experience of being an adult. A further example is the continuing debate about working parents, which tends to focus on how these changes will play out in future adults rather than on how these changes have altered the social structure of childhood.

Good examples of the normal approach to children are abundant. An underlying assumption of traditional studies is that the end justifies the means; that is, producing successful adults is the main criterion for analysis. Treating children as a form of human capital focuses our attention on outcomes rather than on the quality of the everyday life of the child, and treats the stage of childhood as a time to get through or even endure for the sake of certain preferred adult gains.

Studies that link small family size to children's high performances on tests as an indication that small families produce more successful children is an example of adult outcome-based evaluation (Blake, 1989). Leaving aside the difficulty of measuring personal definitions of success, such studies do not tell us anything about how children experience a small family and how they might feel about the absence of siblings. As Qvortrup has argued, "Too long, in my view, have we accepted that the adult world is something to which children must adapt and that socializing measures are directed toward children's futures as adults. This is not a fair deal for children, and I think that advocates for children should be much more conscious about and develop ideas of children's standpoint and children's priorities" (Qvortrup, 1999 p. 54).

Our work is, therefore, guided by two underlying assumptions: that children are entitled to dignity and basic human rights, and that their childhood is a stage that also deserves our attention and respect.

Next, we turn to three basic guidelines that governed the selection of our domains of study and our methods of analysis.

CHILDREN AS A UNIT OF OBSERVATION

If children have basic rights and their childhood is itself worthy of study, then it follows that efforts to measure and monitor children's well-being should make the child the unit of observation. We argue in favor of the need to focus on child-centered indicators, ones that start from the child and move outwards. Traditional data may have determined the child's income by looking at family income--an indicator that, without knowing more about the context, may not tell us much about the child's situation.

Studies of child well-being are often based on data that do not directly assess the child at all. Such studies may select the mother or the family as the unit of analysis. For example, household composition, which focuses on those with whom the child primarily resides, is often used to indicate family structure. Yet from the child's point of view, the primary household may exclude highly significant people in the "child's" concept of her family: a noncustodial parent, grandparent, or others with whom she stays for extended periods of time. This information is lost in traditional surveys. Children are often invisible in statistical reports using social indicators (Jensen & Saporiti, 1992).

Measuring conditions that reflect the care-giving capacity of the child's social environment may be strongly associated with child well-being, but is not the same as measuring the status of the child directly. If analysts are interested in whether children are well-fed, well-housed, and provided sufficient medical care, they must measure these directly. Sen has argued for measures that reflect the life a person is actually living rather than the resources or means a person may have available. Sen's approach takes into account personal choices, constraints, circumstances, and abilities to achieve a preferred living standard. Applying Sen's approach to the assessment of a child's living conditions highlights the need to focus on the child, rather than the household or community, as the unit of analysis. Thus we have agreed on the need for segregated data about children, data that can tell us about such sub-groups of children as those with disabilities, refugees, or children with other minority status.

Sauli has pointed out that in the past children were "hidden" in families, and the state focused on public appearances of children. In addition, since the emphasis in planning is on adults, states are much more likely to have a statistical measure of fathers with resident children than children with resident fathers (Sauli, 1997 p. 289). The implications for understanding childhood and for designing intelligent child-centered policies are enormous. An informative example could be drawn from Sauli's work on families in Finland; looking at families, half the families with children are one-child families, but looking at children, only a quarter of them live without siblings (Sauli, 1997 p. 290).

One area of investigation in which children have become the unit of analysis is that of the child as consumer. Although these efforts are almost exclusively in the private sphere, they are an indication of the new interest on the part of some groups in focusing on the child. Marketing surveys and the resultant media programming aimed at children is highly sophisticated. We need similarly sophisticated research for policies and programs for children in the public sphere.

If we are to have accurate data that reflects our respect for children and their experience, we accept responsibility for developing indicators that focus on the child as the unit of observation. To the extent that we employ traditional data bases, we understand the need to go to the basic data which will help us disaggregate information so that we can reconfigure child centered data for reliable assessment of the state of children's well-being.

EMPHASIS ON POSITIVE INDICATORS

Stemming in part from an emphasis on the adult world, research about children has centered on at-risk youth. Program and funding justifications appear to rely on arguments that address what is wrong in children's lives. The children who receive the bulk of public attention are those who are in trouble. It is not surprising, then, that research has often dwelled on the presence or absence of risk factors rather than on assessment of assets or positive well-being.

Thus, the body of knowledge about children's problems and threats to their survival and development far exceeds what is known about children's strengths, satisfaction, and realization of opportunities. Even measuring the absence of risk factors or negative behaviors differs from measuring the presence of protective factors or positive behaviors (Aber & Jones, 1997). Most of us wish for our children something more than the mere absence of debilitating problems in their lives. Thus, we want to develop positive indicators that can capture the level of well-being and not just the absence of risk.

Especially in light of the desire to produce information that would be useful to policymakers, emphasis on positive indicators of children's well-being is crucial. We argue that policies must aim to accomplish more than the elimination of risks. Such an emphasis merely holds the state accountable for minimum levels of attention to children, levels deemed necessary to prevent or alleviate harmful conditions; it does little to advance the societal responsibility to promote genuine well-being. As Resnick has pointed out,

> children's well-being indicators are on the move from concentrating only on trends of dying, distress, disability and discomfort to tackling the issue of indicators of sparkle, satisfaction and well-being (Resnick, 1995).

Aber and Jones have suggested that part of the difficulty of developing positive indicators lies in our lack of agreement on what constitutes "positive development." They have offered a system of stage-specific developmental tasks that could be used to indicate levels of positive development. As we continue to develop methods of assessing positive development, we remain committed to creating indicators that reflect positive development rather than relying exclusively on those that assess failure.

IMPORTANCE OF SELECTING POLICY-ORIENTED INDICATORS

We strongly believe that a major criterion for selecting indicators is that they be useful for community work and policy makers. Here, we would like to stress the importance of including policy makers in the process of developing the indicators and discussing the usefulness of various choices. Any such effort would draw attention to the importance of child well-being now and in the future. In addition, policy-relevant indicators are more likely to assure that the selection, data collection, and reporting processes will bring public attention to the issues of child well-being that are raised.

Moreover, indicators make possible the evaluation of particular programs and policies, especially over time. Current policies can be examined in light of past efforts and evaluation of proposed changes can be enhanced.

Finally, the data will help reveal gaps in programming or policy development and offer ideas about how to fill them. As conceptualized, the indicators studies, when replicated within and beyond national and regional settings, will elucidate significant differences among groups of children. Data can then be used by child advocates and decision makers to better and more effectively allocate limited resources.

Measuring and monitoring efforts then, in our minds, are based on the asssumptions that the child has basic rights and that childhood is a valuable stage in itself. The selection of indicators must be also guided by an understanding of the significance of focusing on the child as the unit of analysis, of emphasizing positive behavior and conditions, and of remaining policy oriented.

Furthermore, our work has led us to discuss and clarify three controversial issues that arise in designing an effective and reliable measuring and monitoring effort, those issues are presented below.

MONITORING CHILDREN'S RIGHTS VS. MONITORING CHILDREN'S WELL-BEING

Although inspired and to some extent guided by the child rights movement, we would like to clarify some qualitative differences between monitoring rights and monitoring well-being. Perhaps the most crucial difference is the standard used to measure these things. Children's well-being is normally focused on what is desirable, but rights monitoring addresses legally established minimums. These minimums are likely, of course, to change over time and space. The CRC, as we have pointed out, is unlike previous international human rights documents in that it integrates civil and political rights with economic social and cultural rights.

However, the International Covenant on Economic Social and Cultural Rights requires that a ratifying state

> take steps...to the maximum of its available resources, with a view to achieving progressively the full realization of the rights recognized in the present Covenant by all appropriate means... (Article 2).

The language of "progressive" achievement was debated during drafting and was included on the understanding that these rights did not give rise to the same level of immediate obligations as did the obligations in the Civil and Political Rights Covenant, which were required to be fully binding at the moment of ratification.

The language of the CRC follows this pattern, obligating the ratifying states

> with regard to economic, social and cultural rights...to undertake such measures to the maximum extent of their available resources... (Article 4).

Article 27 of the CRC refers

> to a standard of living adequate for the child's physical, mental, spiritual, moral and social development (paragraph 1).

When combined with the language "in accordance with national conditions and within their means" (Paragraph 3), and the language in Article 4, it is clear that there is an expectation that the minimal levels that are acceptable and/or adequate will vary. Such acceptable and expected variance creates a challenge for scholars developing criteria and indicators as they look at differentially endowed states, as well as within a single state over time.

Another significant distinction between monitoring rights and monitoring well-being comes into play as we develop indicators we hope will be of use to legislators and other policy makers. Establishing that rights have been met, or not, will engage us in an exercise that requires clear, concrete, and observable phenomena. Indicators that are abstract and suggestive and even, perhaps, persuasive about children's well-being are less powerful for rights monitoring.

The two activities do share some common features however. The CRC is most fundamentally based on recognizing and enhancing the dignity of the child. Our search for indicators has, therefore, been always conscious of the need to be, at minimum, consistent with a concept of the child and the child's environment that is consonant with the dignity of the child. Our overall concern has also been to give strong consideration to the extent to which various institutions we are examining are likely to promote and enhance the dignity of the child.

Monitoring rights and monitoring well-being also share a focus on child-centered indicators, ones that can be measured at the level of the child. Such indicators draw attention to the actual situation of children and allow for sensitivity to differential treatment of children by race, class, gender, special needs, religion, or minority status. These considerations grow out of the CRC provision that affords children protection from discrimination (Article 2).

A further similarity in the two types of monitoring highlights crucial concepts for interpretation of data for policy makers. The CRC lays heavy emphasis on the standard of the "best interest of the child," which should inform our consideration of law and policy. In addition, the CRC requires that policies be interpreted and applied with due consideration of "the child's evolving capacities" (Article 5).

COMBINING SUBJECTIVE AND OBJECTIVE RESEARCH

As we have noted numerous times already, our work is drawn on that of an international study group, which included participants with highly diverse methodological skills. Yet agreement was easily reached that both quantitative and qualitative research would be necessary for our work. In the discussions about collecting data in new ways and in new domains, as well as in reviewing traditional and existing data, the usefulness of multiple methods was identified.

In addition, based on a widespread agreement, we argue for the necessity of including the perspective of children in whatever research is undertaken.

> Large-scale social phenomena and small-scale inter-
> subjective action implicate each other such that the
> complexity of the social world cannot be expressed
> through a simple asymmetry of objective social
> structure and subjective actors (Prout, 1997 p.96).

Yet, much research on children's lives has until recently been focused on efforts at objective description, treating children as passive objects that are acted upon by the adult world. For example, socialization studies often appeared to assume that the child was a blank slate to be indoctrinated. Current sociological studies focus on children as active members of society, who themselves influence the adults in their lives and their own peers. Youth culture often is co-opted into mainstream adult culture, often through the media.

A number of studies did focus on children. For example, several scholars have conducted in-depth interviews with children about their perceptions of their rights, finding that age, gender, and nationality, among other factors, influence these perceptions (Melton & Limber, 1992).

We argue that in order to gain an accurate measure and provide meaningful monitoring of children's well-being, we need to develop means of gathering children's subjective perceptions of their world and insights into their experiences.

SURVIVAL OR BEYOND?

The basic assumption that initiated our work and that of our international study group was the need to focus on child well-being beyond survival. Much attention has been paid to children's physical survival, and substantial progress has been made in obtaining from national governments commitments to improve the health of their children. Existing research to a great extent now describes where children's survival is threatened. In fact, the collection and publication of data on children's health has stimulated action to provide programs to save children's lives.

Infant and child mortality rates, school enrollment and dropout figures, immunization records and levels of childhood diseases are all examples of data that has been generated to assess the physical status of the child. A fundamental shift occurs when the focus is moved from survival to well-being. Choosing to direct our energies to measuring and monitoring child well-being moves us from efforts to determine minimums, as in saving life, to a next step--the quality of life.

Current information, however, reveals little about the quality of the lives of children in various cultural contexts. Even when looking beyond survival, the data we have may tell us about progress in advancing the health of children--such as how much children have grown--or even educational achievements--such as how well groups of children have performed on tests. This data, though, tells us little about the emotional growth of children, their own perceptions of the quality of their lives, or the process by which children actually learn. With adults, quality-of-life indices typically are composed of multiple measures that take into account life satisfaction and perceptions of needs, priorities, and aspirations. And qualitative data can validate the adequacy and relevance of more objective measures about life beyond survival.

Pittman and Irby (Pittman & Irby, 1997 p. 242) argue that successful adolescence and successful adulthood are based on positive development in a number of key areas: safety and structure; membership and belonging; self-worth/contribution; mastery and sense of purpose; responsibility and independence/interdependence; and self-awareness/spirituality. This is just one list, but it reflects qualitative measures arising from quality-of-life considerations.

In choosing to focus on child well-being beyond survival, we do not ignore the continuing survival issues that plague large and small minorities within developed countries, and many children in other countries. Existing measuring and monitoring has made us more aware of differences between children in different states, but also between groups of children within a single state. Thus, we have learned that there are often grave disparities between groups of children in both rich and poor countries, with some children in the wealthiest countries living in poverty conditions. The effort to draw attention to the very great importance of measuring and monitoring child well-being, then, in no way lessens the importance of ongoing efforts to measure and monitor child survival.

CONCLUSIONS

The underlying philosophy of our project, then, is built upon the assumptions that children are entitled to basic human rights, including economic, social, and cultural rights as well as traditional civil and political rights. We have also accepted the assumption that childhood is a life stage worthy of study independently and in comparison with other life stages.

The selection of domains of study and the indicators that would reveal most about these domains was guided by three principles: the unit of observation is the child; the focus is on positive rather than negative dimensions of children's lives and situations; and the goal is to inform and evaluate programs and policies.

Finally, we appreciate the similarities but also the significant differences between monitoring rights and monitoring well-being. We reject easy distinctions between objective and subjective research, and accept the need for diverse methodologies, including studies of children's own perceptions and experiences; and we hope to contribute innovative insights and perspectives by focusing on indicators of the quality of children's lives beyond survival.

CHAPTER 4

FIVE "NEW" DOMAINS OF CHILDREN'S WELL-BEING

In this chapter, we present the five domains of children's well-being selected by our international study group. The chapter is divided into five sections. First we discuss the need for new domains; then, we turn to the question of why five domains rather than a single theoretical framework. In the third section, we present the context we used for selecting those specific domains. Then, in the fourth section, we present the domains we selected. Finally, in the fifth section, we discuss some implications for choosing indicators within the domains.

THE NEED FOR NEW DOMAINS

There is no doubt that the field of developing indicators of child well-being is going through rapid evolution, accompanied by a number of changes and shifts. An analysis of the field of child well-being indicators based on the various state of the child reports (see Appendix 1 and Chapter 2) and a number of major events[7] and developments led us to the following conclusions.

The field is undergoing four major shifts (i.e.,, from survival to well-being, from negative to positive, from well becoming to well-being, and from traditional to new domains). These shifts are occurring virtually everywhere--although at different paces in different places. The shifts we identified are presented below[8].

---

[7] We refer to the following events: The European Center Project (which is described in length in Chapter 2 of this volume); The Conference on Indicators of Children's Well-being that were held in November, 1994 at Bethesda, Maryland, and the volume that resulted from it under the same title; The International Project on Measuring and Monitoring Children's Well-being (which is described in length in Chapter 2 of this volume); The Luxembourg Income Study Conference on "Child Well-being in Rich and Transition Countries" that was held on September 1999 in Luxembourg; and The Harvard Science Project of the Collaborative Center for Children's Well-being (CCCW)

[8] A thorough review and discussion of those shifts can be found in (Ben-Arieh, forthcoming).

A. Ben-Arieh et al (eds.), Measuring and Monitoring Children's Well-Being, 47–65.
© 2001 *Kluwer Academic Publishers. Printed in the Netherlands.*

From Survival to Well-Being

Increased interest in the state of children--their well-being and their quality of life—has sparked a number of efforts to measure the state of the child in different societies and countries (see Appendix 1). Those efforts have contributed to a shift in the focus on measuring the state of the child. Although a large body of statistical data on the state of children has been published for some time, researchers and professionals working in the field have begun to believe that some new measures and indicators should be devised.

Measures such as infant and child mortality rates, school enrollment, and percentage of children who have been immunized, while still important, nevertheless seem insufficient for measuring the well-being and quality of children's lives today. These measures deal mainly with survival and the basic needs of children, and are inadequate for measuring the state and the quality of the life of children beyond survival. Aber argues that it is time to develop indicators that go beyond the basic needs of development and beyond the phenomenon of deviance (Aber & Jones, 1997). And Pittman and Irby argue for indicators and action beyond survival and prevention in order to promote youth development (Pittman & Irby, 1997).

From 'Negative' to 'Positive'

Attention is beginning to focus on the need for positive indicators of the state of the child as much as negative ones. Measures of the absence of risk factors or negative behaviors are not the same as measures of the presence of protective factors or positive behaviors (Aber & Jones, 1997). For example, the most common measures of early childhood development pertain to deficiencies in achievements, problem behaviors, and negative circumstances. The absence of problems or failures, however, does not necessarily indicate proper growth and success. Pittman and Irby observe that the challenge for policy researchers and advocates is to press for the development of indicators that hold societies accountable for more than the safe warehousing of children and youth. Youth development must be defined and linked securely as both a product of and a contributor to family, community, and economic development (Pittman & Irby, 1997).

Finally, politically, the emphasis on negative indicators or "bad news" without contextual information has led to speculation about causal factors and the tendency to search for blame and punishment. This particular type of politicization contributes to polarization, and fails to serve the interests of children. Thus, the necessity for positive indicators of children's well-being is becoming increasingly evident.

From Well-Becoming to Well-Being

A third shift, although in its infancy, is also starting to occur, as a result of the tension between two schools of thought. One emphasizes the need to concentrate on children's future well-being (i.e.,, on preparing children for a productive and happy adulthood), and the other emphasizes "childhood as a stage in and of itself," with the need to concentrate on the present well-being of children.

As the title of this section suggests, the term *well-being* has been adjusted in our work to describe *present* well-being, whereas the term *well-becoming* is used to describe a future-oriented focus. The European Center Project (see Chapter 2) laid the basis for looking at children's well-being from an intergenerational perspective. In Qvortrup's estimation,

> The conventional preoccupation with the so-called 'next generation' is, however, basically a preoccupation with adults, which is not wrong as such; as a student of childhood, however, I dare venture an interest as well for present childhood as well as future childhood (Qvortrup, 1997 p. 101).

Similarly, Richard de Lone argues that children are instrumentalized by the forward-looking perspective in the sense that their "good life" is postponed to adulthood, and until then they have--as children--opportunities rather than provisions (De Lones, 1979).

Furthermore, by focusing on well-becoming, there is a risk that we do not come to terms with possible conflicts between adulthood and childhood or, if you like, children's and adults' interests. How can we assume that these interests will naturally and always coincide? The more likely probability is that although parents' and children's interests overlap, they cannot be said to coincide.

However, accepting the arguments of Qvortrup and others about the need to concentrate on the well-being of children does not mean denying the relevance of how children develop and become adults. Although the emphasis in monitoring children's well-being ought to shift, and gradually is shifting, to the study of children's everyday lives (including the phenomenology of such experience), this does not mean we should exclude the forward-looking view of the next generation. There is an obvious legitimate societal interest in the healthy socialization of children, and children themselves obviously have a clear interest in the provision of resources in a way that will maximize their future choices.

Both perspectives (children as persons today and children in their future status as older children and ultimately as adults) are legitimate and necessary, both for social science and for public policy. It seems appropriate to maintain a dual perspective–one that is forward-looking as well as one that honors the life world of children as children. However, since the perspective that focuses on children's well-being has been underemphasized in existing indicators efforts, there is room for some major contributions to be made by developing new measures of well-being that derive from this newer perspective.

From 'Traditional' to 'New' Domains

The three shifts described above ultimately contributed to a fourth one. Until recently, when measuring the state of children, researchers concerned themselves with measuring children's basic survival needs; they focused primarily on the deviant and the negative aspects of children lives; and were mainly interested in children's well-becoming.

Looking at children's well-being beyond survival and at positive indicators naturally brings into focus new domains of child well-being and to the creation of new domains of study, such as children's life skills and children's culture.

We now look at why we have decided to focus on five domains of study rather than the development or application of a single unified theory.

WHY FIVE DOMAINS, RATHER THAN A SINGLE UNIFIED THEORY?

It is becoming clear that if measuring children's well-being is to serve a monitoring function, and especially if it is to serve children's interests, it must have enduring importance in various cultures and include short- as well as long-term measures. To be comprehensive, the effort should balance measures across various domains of children's lives, and be carefully constructed to include current and historically excluded subpopulations of children—for example, children with disabilities; indigenous, minority, very poor, or isolated populations; those separated from families; and children who are homeless, refugees, or immigrants (Andrews & Ben-Arieh, 1999).

Furthermore, it is becoming clear that the concept and perception of children's well-being are going through some major changes. A number of efforts[9] are underway around the world trying to define and set forth a unified theoretical framework for children's well-being. Many argue that the CRC should be used as a framework (Andrews & Kaufman, 1999; Hodgkin & Newell, 1998). The proponents of this approach argue, persuasively, that the slow, careful, and committed process by which the Convention was drafted (and the universal ratification of the Convention) give it a special status and make it an excellent framework for measuring and monitoring children's well-being (Verhellen, 1996).

Nevertheless, we found that for the reasons presented in Chapter 3, there are important differences between monitoring rights and monitoring well-being. The Committee on the Rights of the Child and the child advocacy groups involved in preparing the required reports to the Committee are properly focusing their attention on children's rights. Their standards and criteria are qualitatively different from the well-being monitoring we are exploring.

Others argue in favor of accepting the theory of transitions between different stages in life (Avard & Tipper, 1997). Much work is being done on developmental theories of child well-being--especially in regard to psychological development (Limber & Hashima, 1999), but also in regard to physical, social, moral, and spiritual development (Andrews & Kaufman, 1999; Flekkoy & Kaufman, 1997; Flekkoy & Kaufman, 1999; Hodgkin & Newell, 1998; Rushton & Greenberg, 1999; Thompson & Randall, 1999; Torney-Purta, 1999). These transitional or developmental approaches do not claim to provide a total framework for measuring and monitoring, but instead offer a focus on one dimension of the child's life. Often, as well, they take a standard for development based on the preferred adult outcome. Although this is a valid choice, it implies the need to prepare children for their transition into adulthood or to monitor the developmental process, rather than our preferred focus-- to select indicators that focus on the stage of childhood itself.

---

[9] Some of those ongoing efforts are: UNICEF work on trying to conceptualize the term of children's well-being and rights; and The Collaborative Center for Children's Well-being (CCCW) work and especially its Harvard Science group.

Similarly, a number of studies are using the ecological theory as a framework for child well-being (Andrews, 1997) or building a theory around the concept of children in society (Dolev & Habib, 1997). We found both of these approaches to be useful in understanding child well-being, but they were not able to encompass all that we wanted to include so that we could consider the whole spectrum of children's lives.

Thus, as explained in the previous chapter, our project group decided to rely on a number of concepts when selecting the various domains of child well-being, taking into consideration the values we wanted to stress, the desire to remain policy relevant, our understanding of the shifts in the development of social indicators, and our concern with the whole child. We determined that no single theoretical framework would cover all that we felt was needed. In addition, we wanted to be certain that in applying universal concepts of well-being we would have the latitude to remain culturally sensitive. We were concerned that any single unified theory at this point might not be able to address cultural diversity. For all these reasons, we decided to concentrate our work on five domains of children's well-being. We do not mean to suggest that these five domains provide a definitive categorization; for some research objectives, these five may not be the only or even the most important ones.

THE CONTEXT OF "NEW" DOMAINS OF CHILDREN'S WELL-BEING

Although we just argued for focusing on various domains of children's well-being without the need for a theoretical framework, placing the domains within a context will help to clarify our selections and their usefulness. The broader context was presented in the previous chapter. Thus the "new" domains of children's well-being are clearly oriented around children's rights; they consider childhood as a stage of itself; and they are relevant to policies and services for children.

When looking in more depth at the context, we acknowledge that these "new" domains must be responsive to new developments, such as those described earlier in this chapter. Finally, as a consequence of our basic assumptions and guidelines (Chapter 3), we suggest the following context for the new domains of children's well-being, which reflects a need to know more about children's lives and participation in their communities and in the larger society. We see such studies as "snapshots" of children's lives focusing on children's current and ordinary lives, and not intended primarily to tell us anything about the future. The context for these snapshots is represented by answers to a set of questions that will illuminate the nature and content of children's well-being.

The following six questions provide such a context:

1.   What are children doing?

2.   What do children need?

3.   What do children have?

4.   What do children think and feel?

5.   To whom or what are children connected and related?

6.   What do children contribute?

We believe that answering this set of questions will give us a more complete picture of children as human beings in their present life in a way that values them as full members of their community and broader society. In order to answer those questions, we need to focus on new domains of children's life. Much of the data that already exist about currently studied domains would not be of much help in answering this set of questions; thus, we suggest the following set of five new domains

FIVE NEW DOMAINS OF CHILDREN'S WELL-BEING

Our five domains of children's well-being are the following: children's activities, children's economic resources and contribution, civic life skills, personal life skills, and safety and physical status. We will present the rationale behind the selection of these domains, describe their importance, and offer a short analysis of each.

Children's Activities

Across political jurisdictions and cultures, children engage in work, play, creative activities, consumption, social interactions, and other activities that are analogous to adult activities yet qualitatively different. To better understand what children are doing and how they feel about their lives and activities from a child-centered perspective, and to enable their self-fulfillment, empowerment, and life satisfaction, measures must be developed to assess their activities.

Children are active in their families, among peers and community groups; in various social institutions and settings, such as schools, informal educational programs and institutions, and recreation facilities; as consumers and as users and creators of information networks and other media. Indicators in this domain may relate to the extent of engagement in activities, the nature of the activities, places in which these activities occur, and children's perceptions of the relative importance and contribution of the different activities to their lives.

Children's activities and dimensions of time use
Children's everyday activities are diverse and varied, and can be characterized along a variety of dimensions of time use. We propose the following categories as a preliminary scheme for classifying activities:
- Personal care: such as eating, dressing, grooming etc.
- Productive activities, which fall into five different categories: school work, personal creative work, paid work, care of others, domestic or household work, and other activities that contribute to the community. Social interaction - interacting socially with others not for productive purposes (such as "hanging out", listening to music, talking, etc.)
- Leisure\recreation: play, sports, reading, watching television, arts and crafts, etc.
- Transportation time
- Consumption
- Sleep
- Spiritual activities

In labeling some activities as *productive* we do not intend to imply that those not so labeled are without value. However, we have chosen to call those children's activities productive when they have a functional equivalence with adult activities that are generally understood as making a social or economic contribution (see, for example, Qvortrup, 1995).

We further propose the following dimensions of time use for characterizing these activities:

- Duration
- Frequency
- Place, including locations and different institutional settings
- People who are present/participate
- Extent of structure
- Extent of obligation vs. voluntary participation
- Control over content and structure
- Subjective evaluation

The needs for time-use studies

Some of these activities (such as schooling) have gained much attention in terms of their outcomes or consequences. But little research has been conducted regarding the patterns of children's everyday activities and the way in which different patterns of activity affect children's well-being (Ennew, 1994). Thus, there are few existing indicators that may serve to monitor children's well-being, and these indicators do not generally describe patterns of activities.

Systematic up—to-date information concerning children's activities is unavailable in most countries (Gershuny, 1995). Therefore, the measures of these activities need to be developed and refined based on the existing but scattered efforts to collect such data in different countries and across different age groups (see, for example, Plewis, Creeser, & Mooney, 1990). Due to the relatively innovative nature of such inquiries, it is also difficult to point out the different ways in which these patterns are related to child well-being. These relationships will need to be determined in course of developing the measures.

Most of the measures that are proposed in Chapter 5 are based on time-use surveys of children, similar to those already conducted for adults. Data from these surveys will enable us to describe the shape and form of children's daily activities and will provide a basis for comparison among communities and countries that vary in their economic conditions, culture, social organization, and policies toward children. In addition, such data are essential for providing information about similarities and differences in daily activity among children who differ by social class, gender, age, ethnicity, geographic regions, disability, etc.

Developing such measures will help to identify the forces that contribute to shaping children's lives, and the way in which these various forces are related to child well-being, satisfaction, and development.

Children's Economic Resources and Contribution

The impact of economic conditions on children and their lives cannot be ignored. Economic resources available for children play a critical role in enabling them to enjoy life as well as to develop. But children are not merely an economic burden on society (or the family). Children are also an economic resource, active actors and contributors within their households or societal economies. In essence, we think that in order to know what children have as well as what they think and feel, and especially what they contribute, one must look at their economic resources and contribution.

It is our impression that economists and economic research do not focus much on children and childhood. If they do attend to children, the children are viewed as objects, as consumers, and as future adults; they are almost never viewed as subjects and human beings. Abundant economic literature on education and the development of human capital underlines this traditional utilitarian way of thinking. There are a number of studies on childhood in modern societies, which are focused on the cost of children, but only a few studies about children's activities and their economic contributions.

There are however two more recent trends in economic reasoning about childhood: one developed out of asking about the consequences of implementing children's rights for macroeconomic policies. The other is an attempt to elaborate on the economic dimension of childhood as a social category and hence to consider age or generation a relevant economic dimension. Both implementing children's rights as well as establishing a generational approach to childhood in social and economic theory were two recognized goals of our international project, and served as a part of our basic assumptions and guidelines (see Chapter 3).

Macro-economic policies and the rights of the child.
Macro-economic policies and children's rights (or rather their neglect) were, in the past, topics mainly discussed in connection with structural adjustment in developing countries. Stefan de Vylder illustrates the impact of economic policies on the situation of children with a set of concentric circles. At the hub are policies and legislation that explicitly target children--for example, public provision of primary health and education, daycare centers, and regulations against exploitive child labor practices.

In the next circle are policies and institutions that have a strong, but more indirect effect, and which are basically mediated through their impact on the child's family and parents. Here, de Vylder includes tax and public expenditure policies, social security and welfare policies, housing, labor market and family policies. In a third circle are general policies that may have a strong impact but one that is even more indirect, such as trade and exchange rate policies, monetary policies, European integration and globalization etc. In conclusion, there are only a few policy arenas with an explicit childhood focus; there are no macroeconomic policies that are "child-neutral" (De Vylder, 1998).

Structural adjustment programs have their greatest impact on the most vulnerable population groups--women and children in particular. Yet we note growing awareness of children's visibility, and consequently an increasing number of political appeals to provide support for children, to make children's needs a priority, or in any case not to decrease public expenditures for children in periods of stagnation or recession (Parliamentary Assembly of the Council of Europe, 1996). General declarations that children are the future of society are obviously not a sufficient condition for protecting and meeting children's needs; however, explicit programs, such as the South African Children's Budget, may indicate a serious political intention to make children a priority. The next step must be to monitor whether and to what extent budgets follow recommended policies, and follow them in a manner that directly improves child well-being.

Age and generation in economic theory
Macroeconomic developments influence the wealth of a society as a whole, but equally important to our work is the fact that macroeconomic developments affect the distribution of wealth according to class, gender, and age (or generation). We refer to the latter as *generational distributive justice*. We consider two dimensions: expenditures on children (how much parents, governments, other social institutions, and children spend on children) and child poverty (which resources are and are not available to children).

In addition to theoretical debates about analyzing the costs of a child, there is empirical research on the cost of children. Distinctions are made between different types of costs, e.g., standard or minimum costs, direct and theoretical costs (Renard, 1985), public and private costs, etc. Due to different administrative boundaries and budgeting procedures in different countries, it is often difficult to gather comparable data concerning public spending on children across countries. In any case, we would encourage research that would enable us to construct itemized tables of public and private expenditures on different age groups (children and youth, adults and elderly persons).

Data on child poverty has been collected in North America and most European countries (see, for example, Cornia & Danziger, 1997). For most developed countries, child poverty is statistically correlated with (1) the number of children and (2) the number of incomes per household. Again, there might be difficulties in combining the different findings within and among countries due to differences in equivalency scales. How does one accurately compare the income levels of households of different size in different economic settings? In that regard, the OECD scale, counting the first adult as 1,0, the second as 0,7, and each child under 16 as 0,5 is the most widely used and recognized.

Furthermore, distinctions must be made between absolute and relative poverty, and between generational poverty measures (i.e.,, the absolute extent of resources available to children) on one hand, and those referring to the situation of children in relation to the general population on the other hand. The two concepts deal with different dynamics; whereas absolute poverty is about the transmission of poverty from parents to children, relative generational poverty deals with the poverty risk transmitted by children.

Generational distributive justice should not, however, be separated from the *generational division of labor*. In a social-historical perspective, the economic evolution of childhood may be traced back by using as criteria their predominant pertinence to the spheres of either production or consumption on one hand, and their perception as either subjects or objects of the other. Traditional and early child labor, human capital, children as sentimental assets, children as active consumers are all the result of significant transformations brought about by the industrial revolution, school reforms, and the sentimentalization of childhood (Zelizer, 1994) or by looking at the globalization of the free market and the targeting of children as consumers (Hengst, 1998).

A final consideration in this domain deals with the study and identification of the role children fulfill in their family and broader community and the contributions they make to their family, community, and economy.

Civic Life Skills

Children can develop social and civic responsibilities even in their early years, learning cooperation and participation in families and limited environments and gradually expanding their participation in accord with their evolving capacities. Indicators in this domain should measure the extent and level to which children have acquired or exercise self-expression, knowledge about and participation in legal and civic activities, understanding and respect for the rights of others, and genuine tolerance of diversity (Torney-Purta, 1999).

In our context, this domain serves to answer the questions of what children are doing; what children think and feel; to whom or what children are connected and related; and what children contribute. This domain is heavily culture contingent and values oriented; clearly, we have accepted democracy as a guiding value of our work as well as the concept of children's rights and participation (see Chapter 3). Finally, this domain will have to be carefully adjusted, not only to different cultures but also to different age groups within the childhood range (0-18), and in some cases to gender differences among children.

The preamble to the CRC emphasizes the importance of state action to provide children with the protection and assistance needed so that they can

> fully assume (their) responsibilities within the community.

Further, the preamble states the overall goal that

> the child should be prepared to live an individual life
> in society, and be brought up in the spirit of the ideals
> proclaimed in the Charter of the United Nations and
> in particular in the spirit of peace. dignity, tolerance,
> freedom, equality and solidarity.

Taken together, these sections emphasize the importance of participation, which in Articles 12, 13, and 14, the CRC makes a matter of right for children.

Participation is an expression of individual autonomy and thus is basic to respect for a child's personhood. At the same time, participation is the critical ingredient in community, and thus is necessary for protection of children's interests in society. Indeed, there may be no right more fundamental to the protection of children's dignity than that of participation. Furthermore, the significance of participation is obvious in the various settings of which children are a part (not merely those that have an overt civic purpose), including those primarily or exclusively involving children's activities and their peers. Participation in decisions affecting the individual life of the child is also a crucial step in developing genuine participation. Involvement in health care decisions, curriculum decisions, judicial decisions affecting the child, and day-to-day family life decisions are examples of participation that may be actively encouraged with appropriate adjustment to the evolving capacity of the child.

Children's civic skills and involvement are important in contributing to children's sense of their own efficacy and therefore have immediate meaning in children's lives. Yet these skills and participation also have important long-term community, national, and global significance because of the need to socialize children into the knowledge, skills, values, and attitudes that are fundamental to democracy. With the rapid but fragile democratization that is taking place across the globe in recent years (Potter, Goldblat, Kiloh, & Lewis, 1997), the importance of monitoring the presence and development of democratic attributes and skills among children is obvious.

Studies have shown that such skills, as well as the perception of oneself as a citizen whose views are worthy of consideration and one who has the potential to shape public action, does not come naturally, especially among disadvantaged groups (Melton & Limber, 1992; Melton & Saks, 1985). The fact that political ideologies and concepts are starting to become established in the elementary school years (Melton & Limber, 1992) shows the long-term importance of focusing on civic education and skills during the early years of childhood, as well as the need for monitoring levels of knowledge, participation, and effects.

As John Dewey argued, democracy is primarily a way of life, rather than a form of government (Stuhr, 1998). Therefore, we should focus not only on children's direct political knowledge and skills, but also on their involvement in family, local community, schools, and civil society as a whole.

Personal Life Skills

Children must develop skills to contribute to their own well-being, including self-esteem and assertiveness and the capacity to learn and work. These could be assessed through culturally relevant measures of education and achievement. Such measures should include the ability to initiate and maintain social interactions, the extent and level of self-esteem, self-efficacy, and other emotional capacities, work-related skills, the ability to maintain a healthy lifestyle, and skills required to be a wise consumer (Flekkoy & Kaufman, 1999).

Much work has been carried out around the world on those aspects of children lives and well-being. Personal life skills have been defined in some studies as adaptive and positive behaviors to deal effectively with challenges of everyday life. Others have used different definitions or categorizations. In our context, the personal life skills domain serves to answer the following questions: What do children need? What do children have? What do children think and feel? And to whom or what are children connected and related? Once again we must note that this domain would have to carefully adjusted to different cultures, to different age groups, and in many cases to gender differences among children.

Children, as active participants in their environments, use personal life skills as they respond to life's opportunities and challenges. Life skills competence allows them to contribute to their own well-being. These skills should be appropriate for the child's developmental capacity, culture, and ability level (including age, disability, or special need).

A child's capacity to learn or use life skills is affected by several factors, including the child's perceptions and ability. Additionally, environmental factors will elicit or inhibit children's personal life skills. Thus indicators of children's life skills must include perceptual, behavioral, and environmental measures.

Self-esteem, self-efficacy, expectations about educational attainment, expectations about life goals, and motivation all can have an impact on the acquisition and use of personal life skills. Behaviorally, children need skills such as wellness behaviors, choice of nutritional food and diet (when available), regular physical exercise, adequate rest, attention to safety and avoidance of hazards for responding to all aspects of life.

Social skills like communication (listening, assertiveness, conflict management) and engaging in mutual support are necessary in order to develop secure relationships with family, peers, and community members. Children can also acquire knowledge to understand parents and prepare themselves for parenthood.

Emotional and behavioral skills, such as coping, that help a child face adversity, solve problems, and respond to challenges, and remain resilient are no less important. Children must regulate their behavior in different ways according to setting, such as being boisterous on the playground and not in the classroom, rather than vice versa. Practicing socially responsible behavior such as sexual responsibility and resistance to alcohol, tobacco, or other drug abuse and avoiding crime are also indicators of well-being. Finally, the exercise of creative abilities helps the child achieve life satisfaction, and academic skills help a child read, write, and calculate numbers and gain access to community resources and career opportunities.

As children live in their physical and social environments, their well-being is enhanced by access to opportunities that help them learn or practice developmentally appropriate skills. When faced with adversity, children need environmental supports such as safe places, social support, and mental health care. Children benefit from a sense of balance among the various life skills. For example, a child who must devote exceptional energy to mastering emotional states because of chronic exposure to danger may be able to give less energy to the exercise of academic or physical wellness skills. Or a child who spends 80 percent of his or her waking hours on academic activities is likely to suffer in the other areas. A child's well-being is therefore contingent on keeping a balance in life.

Safety and Physical Status

Safety and physical status are commonly thought of as the most basic components of well-being. A child who is not safe will likely neither live nor develop in an optimal way, and may also be more vulnerable to physical injury and trauma.

Surveys of children and youth in many cultures often reveal that their primary concern is their safety. Millions of children live in threatening circumstances due to family violence, community violence, sexual exploitation, war and civil conflict, or their own institutionalization, homelessness, or refugee status. Even more children are threatened by inadequate health or mental health care. Measures can determine the extent to which children live under such conditions and the children's perceptions and expectations regarding their physical status and safety.

In our context, this domain serves to answer the following questions: What do children need? What do children have? And what do children think and feel? It is evident that around the issues of safety and physical status the dispute on survival or beyond is the most relevant. Clearly, most of the world child population still has to cope with a threat to their mere survival. Thus, it seems hard to concentrate on aspects of trauma and safety perceptions when millions of children's are coping with under-5 mortality rates or unbelievable rates of HIV infection. Nevertheless, as we made clear in our introduction, we know those issues to be central to the lives of millions of children in industrialized countries. We also recognize their utility in serving as a better aspiration for all the world's children.

Safety
Safety has been defined as those aspects of well-being that are affected by biological, physical, and environmental threats. Our domain framework is based on a structural-ecological approach put forth most recently by Aber (Aber, 1997). Because child and adolescent safety is affected by macro forces at the municipal, regional, and national levels, neighborhood conditions and organization, and family characteristics and processes, our approach to defining the domain focuses on these relationships.

Since violence at all levels has severe affects on children's well-being, it is important to include perceptions of children and parents of the safety of children in their immediate settings and the vulnerability of children to violence as well as the general level of neighborhood or community safety. A growing problem in a number of industrialized countries is school safety, and here it would be important to include perceptions of children, teachers, and parents about the degree of safety in schools.

Substance abuse (and especially illegal substance abuse) may be one characteristic of unsafe environments and may lead to violent behavior against other youth or adults; it is highly correlated with juvenile delinquency[10]. Substance abuse affects peer relationships and family functioning as well as physical and mental health and as such can be seen as one example of the need for a broadly defined concept of children's safety.

Health Status

Although the broad approach to safety applies to health as well, we make use of more traditional health indicators here and employ a service research approach. Indicators on the health status of children are abundant, even though there are some notable areas, including mental health, which are in need of indicator development. The adequacy of services in terms of quality, availability, and accessibility is an area that is quite underdeveloped- -not only in the measurement of these constructs, but also in their definition.

IMPLICATIONS FOR CHOOSING INDICATORS

The domains of children's well-being should adequately portray the range and diversity of children's experiences by examining disaggregated data as well as centralizing tendencies. Quantifiable and qualitative measures should address children's behaviors and the structures of which they are a part. They should be grounded in theory and research that meet the tests of valid and reliable measurement (Moore, 1995; Moore, 1997).

The final selection of the indicators in the various domains must also be guided by principles that address the purpose and scope of the measuring and monitoring process as well as the accuracy of measurements.

It is important to note that the selection of indicators should be contingent on culture, age, gender, and specific needs of specific populations. In many cases, we can see the usage of the same indicator or measurement for several groups of children who differ by culture, age, or gender. In others, specific indicators would have to be composed for different groups of children. But in all cases, we foresee a need for taking all of this into account when analyzing the data collected and when trying to draw implications from the indicators and the data.

---

[10] The research supports a correlation between illegal drug and substance abuse and juvenile delinquency. There is no support for such correlation between legal substance abuse (as tobacco) and juvenile delinquency.

Finally, one must remember that the domains by themselves do not provide definitive criteria for selecting the specific indicators of children's well-being. The options for operationalization also play a major role in choosing the indicators. Thus, immediately after presenting our suggested indicators within those five domains, we follow up with a chapter devoted to discussing how we might measure and monitor children's well-being and the possible sources of information we might use.

CHAPTER 5

POSSIBLE INDICATORS OF CHILDREN'S WELL-BEING

Any effort to monitor and measure children's well-being is contingent on finding and using the right measures for the task. As a result of earlier work, it seemed appropriate to contribute to this ongoing effort by opening up new domains and concentrating on aspects of well-being beyond survival and positive development of children (see Chapters 3 & 4). Thus, in this chapter, we suggest lists of indicators as an addition to and not a replacement for existing domains and indicators of children's well-being.

Obviously there are many more possible indicators. We do not mean to under estimate any one of them. Rather, we are confident that the indicators we choose are an additional contribution for the effort to measure and monitor the state of children as a step toward improving their well-being.

This chapter presents a list of some fifty indicators of children's well-being. This list is the final product of the international project. The indicators are divided into the five domains of children's well-being described in Chapter 4. They all adhere to our basic assumptions and approach elaborated in Chapter 3, and are discussed and presented relative to the practical ways they could be measured as elaborated in Chapter 6.

Thus, this chapter has seven sections. This brief preamble is followed by five sections, each of them devoted to one of our five domains of children's well-being. In each section, a short introduction is presented followed by the list of indicators. Each indicator is presented with a short rationale and a discussion as to how it could be measured. The final section of the chapter presents some short conclusions.

We began with a much more divergent list and have narrowed the range to decrease fragmentation. The list of indicators presented below contains indicators at different levels (and nature). Some of those differences have been handled in the process of finalizing the list; others have remained in order to address different aspects of children's lives, although it may mean the use of different methods of collecting data. Furthermore, some overlap among different domains still exists. We see this as a positive consequence

A. Ben-Arieh et al (eds.), Measuring and Monitoring Children's Well-Being, 67–90.
© 2001 *Kluwer Academic Publishers. Printed in the Netherlands.*

of trying to integrate different approaches for measuring children's well-being. This is also an outcome of accepting the possibility that traditional methods of data collection may not be satisfactory and the need for relying on a variety of sources of information and on different research methods.

It is possible that the entire set of indicators will not always be used as a whole and that some would like to concentrate on a specific domain or group of indicators. In such a situation, the slight overlap between indicators will be helpful since it supports a broader view of each domain, thus enabling a better picture (even if still partial) of children's lives.

Finally, the indicators are presented with regard to the entire child population in a universal way. This should not be seen as implying that the same indicators should be used for all the children of the world regardless of their culture, age, gender, or specific need or population group. We have made it clear from the beginning that our work was dominated by the western culture (see the Introduction). We have also made it clear that we recognize the need for being culture contingent and age and gender sensitive. But we believe much of that adaptation and sensitivity should be addressed in the process of devising the measurement tools and especially during the interpretation of the data. We have argued that dividing the child population while looking at the concepts or even while looking at indicators and measurements in general would be harmful for children's well-being and their cause as a distinct population group (see Introduction and Chapters 3 and 4).

CHILDREN'S ACTIVITIES

Six indicators are suggested in this domain. It is worth repeating that the children's activities domain is unique when compared to the other four domains (see Chapter 4). As a result of its unique character, its basic source of information is time-use measurements. The indicators proposed are based on a time-use survey of children, similar to those already conducted for adults. This methodology, derived mainly from anthropology and sociology, will enable us to describe the scope and form of children's daily activities.

Furthermore, the indicators suggested here should be seen as measurements. Due to the fact that all of them are culturally contingent, we are suggesting them as means for assessing the status of children, but the interpretation of the findings should be carefully done in accordance with the age group, gender, and the particular culture.

We do not underestimate the magnitude of resources required to carry out such studies or the need to carefully consider a large number of complex methodological issues that will arise in the process of operationalizing the suggested measurements. However, developing such measures will facilitate a discussion that will in turn lead to a better understanding of the forces that shape children's lives and the way in which these are related to their well-being.

All six indicators could be measured by using time-use studies, and a number of approaches for undertaking such studies exist. Time-use data could be collected using time dairies carefully completed by trained observers. The children themselves could complete the time-use diaries and time use could be studied through surveys asking a sample of caregivers, parents, and children about their time use and daily activities[11].

Each of those methods has its advantages and disadvantages. Each of them can be used in order to obtain the needed data on our suggested indicators; the only restriction is that the child's perspective on his or her time use and daily activities must be taken into account.

Distribution of children's time across types of activities
Around the world, there are continuing debates concerning the optimal time that a child should spend in various activities. Although a broad range of time distributions can be equally beneficial to children's well-being, it is important to ascertain the optimal ranges of time that should be spent in various activities, and the magnitude of deviations that lead to harm. For example, though most policies aimed at enhancing educational attainment generally involve increasing the amount of time children devote to school-related activities, there is currently no information that indicates the point of diminishing returns compared to such other time uses as play, work, or socializing.

Percentage of time spent in productive activities (school, paid work, household work, and contributing to community)
Children are generally considered as not only unproductive but also as a burden to society. At best, children's value is referred to in terms of investment. This way of viewing children's productivity results in seeing them as dependent and incompetent, by denying their participation in

---

[11] A good review of existing methods and on time use studies can be found in Larson, 1999 as well as in Ben-Arieh and Ofir, 2000.

society. Reconceptualizing the meaning of productivity in relation to children and indicating the amount of time children actually invest in productive activities may   change this perspective. Furthermore, as elaborated in the section on civic life skills, time spent on so-called nonproductive activities is a vital component of child well-being.

Percentage of time spent in obligatory vs. voluntary activities
Children's participation in civic and community activities, as well as in procedures that affect their lives, is increasingly being recognized as an essential dimension of their well-being (Hodgkin & Newell, 1998). Participation requires opportunities for children to build capacities and exercise skills in taking initiative and responsibility and assuming leadership. Both the amount of time that children spend in activities of their own choice and the varying degrees of control they have in determining the structure and content of these activities are indicators of the extent of these opportunities. Changes in the levels of both these measures with increase with age and will determine the extent to which the social structure provides opportunities for children to exercise their evolving capacities. Although this is also further discussed in the section on the civic life skills domain, we wanted to reemphasize the importance of learning the child's perspective while using this measurement. We find it most important to use the children's interpretation as to the obligatory and voluntary nature of their activities.

Distribution of children's time with different participants (with family, alone, with other children, with other adults or other children and adults)
 Some of the more important issues that have been debated in relation to child well-being have to do with the time that children spend with other people. One important issue has been that of intergenerational relationships (Qvortrup, 1994). It has been argued that children spend more and more time with other children without the presence of adults or in the presence of only a few adults. A related argument has been that changing employment patterns and social structures have resulted in children spending less time with their parents. In light of the public debate concerning these and related issues, it is important to establish whether these changes are actually taking place and to try to determine their effect on children's well-being.

Percent of time spent in places not designated specifically for children
Recent analyses of trends in childhood have suggested that children in modern societies spend increasing amounts of time either in institutions (such as school or after-school programs) specifically designed for them or in the family home. It is suggested that this leads to a sequestration of children and a distancing of children from the wider society.

Children's activities measures would provide information on this point. One particular aspect of this is the independent use by children of the spaces and places in neighbourhood environments, such as the street and shopping areas. It is suggested that children's use of these spaces is related to their well-being--although the direction of influence may be related to other local factors. In areas where the local environment is a safe one, children's use of it may be important in their individual and collective development. In unsafe areas, children's use of the local environment may be related to, for example, levels of injury, exposure to and involvement in criminal activities. As with some of the previous indicators mentioned, this indicator has some overlap mainly with the safety subdomain and its indicators.

Distribution of children's time by satisfaction levels
This is a direct measure of subjective well-being routinely collected for adults in surveys across the industrialized world. It is, however, not generally collected from children. It would provide information with which to compare adult evaluations of children's activities with those of children themselves. It would also, through disaggregation, enable the comparison of satisfaction of children living in different circumstances and allow for international comparisons.

CHILDREN'S ECONOMIC RESOURCES AND CONTRIBUTION

One can hardly exaggerate the importance of economic status and resources for children's well-being. Various studies in various disciplines (i.e.,, economics, social work, psychology, public health, and more) has shown the importance of available economic resources for child well-being. Naturally our list includes a number of indicators on children's economic resources.

As discussed in Chapter 4, we have decided to take a slightly different approach than the conventional one: We argue that children are not merely an economic burden on society (or the family), but are themselves an economic resource and furthermore, are actors and contributors within their households or the broader economy (Wintersberger, 1997). The approach is spelled out in the suggested list of indicators. In order to better handle the task of presenting the indicators and dealing with the various dimensions of this broad and important domain we have decided to divided the domain into four subdomains (i.e.,, macroeconomics and distributive justice, expenditures on children, access to resources, and children's contribution and autonomy).

As a consequence of this focus, we suggest indicators that vary by nature and by point of view. Some of the indicators are based on more traditional economic measures. Others are based on children's perception of their economic status and resources. The rest are a combination of economic measures that are applied to "new" directions and toward different distributional habits and units of observation.

Macroeconomic and Distributive Justice

Macroeconomics describes the wealth of society as a whole and the distribution of resources by class, ethnicity, gender, or age. It is evident that children's well-being is affected by their macro-economic context. The following three indicators are intended to measure how macroeconomic and distributive policies are contributing or harming children's well-being.

Share of equalized income quintiles represented by each age group
By using a common economic measure--equalized income quintiles--for studying differences by age group, we can gain knowledge of our children's well-being compared to other age groups in the society. In fact, employing this traditional indicator in this new way enables us to learn about our children's economic status, not compared to a generalized social norm but rather in comparison to others in the same society. If we accept the notion of children's rights and childhood as a stage of itself, then we must accept the children's entitlements to an equal share of society's wealth.

Relative child poverty rates before and after taxation and transfers
Ample evidence and research exist on the consequences of living in poverty for child well-being (Cornia & Danziger, 1997; Danziger, Danziger, & Stern, 1997; Duncan & Brooks-Gunn, 1997). Poverty itself can be defined and measured by using a variety of methods. In short, one can distinguish between *absolute* and *relative* measurements. The first is based on a key assumption that there is an absolute minimum level of income that a family

needs in order to provide necessary resources for its children. The latter takes into consideration the economic resources a child or family has in relation to other children or families in the given society (Citro & Michael, 1995; Doron, 1980).

We have decided to use relative poverty measurements as an indicator of children's well-being for a number of reasons. First, the mere acceptance of a beyond-survival approach leads to rejecting the adequacy of a minimum standard of living approach. Second, a child rights perspective requires, as a matter of social justice, the equitable distribution of resources among equal human beings. Such an approach dictate the use of relative measurement. Finally, the relative measurement is much more widely used as the "formal" poverty measurement in most of the developed world (Atkinson, Rainwater & Smeeding, 1995; Smeeding, O'Higgins, & Rainwater, 1990).

Percentage of public expenditures by age groups
The third indicator of this subdomain is intended to enrich our knowledge about investment in children, and especially about their share of the public expenditures. Once again, we believe that child well-being is enhanced when children receive an equal share of the public expenditures as compared to other age groups. It is worth noting also that such an indicator would be useful in measuring shares of public expenditures by gender or by age, ethnic, or religious groups.

Expenditures on Children

The last indicator mentioned above serves as a good lead into this subdomain, in which we would like to contribute to knowledge about the extent of resources spent on children--not only public resources, but also private resources within the household. Such a measure could serve as a powerful tool for monitoring children's well-being, especially over time. The trend could show whether more resources or less are spent on children and thus indicate their well-being. Furthermore, such a measure could indicate the relative well-being of children (by age, gender, ethnicity, or religion).

Average costs of children (for the household and for society) by age group
As complicated as it might be, a measure of the "cost of a child" is a vital indicator for understanding children's well-being. A number of studies on the issue have been carried out in recent years (Percival & Harding, 1999). It is evident from them and from other studies that the "cost" of a child is

related to her or his well-being. It is also an excellent indicator for studying the well-being of children from different groups as mentioned above.

Percentage of family expenditures (spent by or on) by children
As a part of the "cost" of the child (measurement) and as an complementary measure, this suggested indicator is more direct in comparing the cost of the child to the cost of other members of the family. Such an indicator is an excellent example of how an indicator should use the child, rather than the family or household, as a unit of observation. In using the family approach, one might find a family spending a lot of money—suggesting a high cost for the child—yet, it may be that none of it is being spent on the family's children. The child in such a family would be worse off a child who lives in a family that spends much less overall but a larger share on the child.

Access to resources

This third subdomain is a natural continuation of its two predecessors. Here, we try to go a step further and look not only at children's share of resources or expenditures, but also on their access to those resources. It is complementary to the previous subdomains because it is not intended to measure actual resources that were allocated or spent on children, but rather to measure the availability of the resources, even if they were never used.

Measures of children's share of the family's material and economic resources
A family's material and economic resources are usually more extensive than what is spent or used. We know from adults that their well-being is affected by the knowledge of what resources are available for them even if they have never used them. We argue that children's well-being is affected in a similar way. Thus, learning about the resources available to children will contribute to our understanding of their well-being.

Undoubtedly, it will be a difficult indicator to measure. First one would have to deal with the issue of how resources can be measured and estimated (some examples could be savings or credit lines that children and youth possess). Then the question follows of how the child's share might be assessed. Finally, any effort to measure availability, before the actual usage of the resource, is bound to be methodologically complicated. However, if it could be done; it would probably require some self-reporting survey asking all members of the family about their perceived share of the family resources. The findings would have to be analyzed with an understanding of the actual expenditure patterns of the family.

Access to various social, educational, and health services regardless of economic status
Finally, the availability of various social services for children is a critical component of their well-being (Kamerman & Kahn, 1997). Controlling for the economic status of children as an intermediate variable would be important to assess access to services. Therefore, we suggest that the best indicator would be access to identified services regardless of the child's economic status. In other words, we would want to ask whether the services (such as immunization, education, and leisure time activities) are available to children, and to what extent the child's economic status represents a possible obstacle to access.

The data about this indicator could be gathered at a number of levels. First, the self-reports of children and their caregivers and parents would be a vital source of information. Administrative data on the take-up levels of various services can be used. Finally, analyzing the legal status and the child's rights to various services would be an important contribution to understanding their well-being.

Children's Contribution and Autonomy

It is important to state clearly that although someone might decide to use only one or some of our five domains of children's well-being, it would not be appropriate to pick and choose among our subdomains, especially between the sub-domains in the children's economic resources and contribution domain.. We have already stressed a number of times the fact that we see children not only as an economic burden or cost but also as contributors to society. This explains why we place such importance on this specific subdomain and its indicators.

Benefits/transfers paid directly to children or to families on behalf of children Benefits represent a simple indicator, which could be measured by using either administrative data or household income surveys. We know that in virtually all the industrialized countries (the welfare states), there are public benefits that are paid to the family on behalf of the child. If a child's well-being is affected by being a contributor as well as a beneficiary, then such a measurement will enrich our knowledge of her or his well-being.

Sources of income of children
We know very little about the economic contribution of children. There may be some instances in which the well-being of children who are working in order to contribute to their family's income and their work suffers. A typical example might be the extensive child and youth labor in developing countries or when a child goes to work instead of attending school. An even more extreme case is when a child sells her or his body for money. We have to know more about how much children contribute to their families, but also what activities are the bases for the contribution. This indicator could be measured through income surveys of children, as is done with adults. Furthermore some data on this indicator may be collected by using administrative data on wages.

Percentage of family resources contributed by children
In addition to knowing how children earn their income, it is important to know how much they are actually contributing. It is worth noting that we prefer using the term resources and not income, in order to emphasize the fact that we are not limiting our focus to cash contribution. Children particularly contribute in-kind resources to their family, for example by babysitting their siblings or doing housework. These activities could be measured through time-use studies, as was previously mentioned, or by conducting surveys on families' resources.

Children's perception of their contribution to the family resources
Finally, as is becoming more and more evident, the child's perception is just as important as any "objective" measurement. It is especially important for our goal of measuring child well-being, due to the evident connections between perceptions and personal well-being.

CIVIC LIFE SKILLS

Concentrating on children's civic skills is vital for their well-being, both because of its immediate meaning in children's lives and their participation in long-term community, national, and global political life. We need to learn to what extent children are acquiring the knowledge, skills, values, and attitudes that are fundamental to democracy. Most work in the field of children's well-being has tended in the past to concentrate mainly on personal life skills (our next domain). However, we believe that concentration on civic life skills is a unique contribution of our project. Measuring and assessing children's civic life skills and thus their well-being is drawing into our work experiences and studies done mainly in law and psychology. In many cases, the measures would have to be based on some kind of legislative or policy analysis. For others knowledge could be gained through attitude surveys and administrative data on the existence of specific mechanisms for children's civic involvement and the value to children of these activities.

Recent years has brought an intense concentration on issues of child participation (Flekkoy & Kaufman, 1997; Flekkoy & Kaufman, 1999), we acknowledge the importance of participation for child well-being, but strive for a broader perspective. These perspective looks on children's attitudes and values as well as on adult societal attitudes. We are also concerned with the opportunities that exist for child civic involvement. Thus we have decided to divide this domain into three subdomains. i.e., civic/community values and awareness, civic/community activities, and opportunities for civic/community activities.

Civic and Community Values and Awareness

By its nature, this subdomain, which focuses on indicators that measure values and awareness, has to rely on surveys and self-reports as its basic source of data.

Percentage who report an interest in current events and in social problems
The basic idea behind suggesting this specific indicator is that civic awareness is a vital component of children's well-being in democratic societies. This is so not only because society needs its children to be aware and involved, but also because children themselves see this as a very important aspect of their well-being (Melton & Limber, 1992). Not being aware can negatively affect well-being.

As we have noted above, to study awareness we would have to rely for information on self- reporting. However, we should be sensitive enough to make sure that our surveys deal with all children in a variety of age groups and cultural settings.

Degree of support for tolerance and expression of minority views and other forms of civil rights
With Western societies becoming more and more heterogeneous, and especially with the emerging issue of minority rights around the world, the importance of this indicator cannot be exaggerated. Using such an indicator

as a measure of child well-being makes a very clear statement. There is more to child well-being than only securing a safe and happy life. Morality and values count as well. If we believe in children's rights, then we must accept that such a belief is an indicator of child well-being. If we believe there is an appropriate way of living--and that some attitudes are desirable while others should be rejected, then we must understand that the presence of such values among our children is an indicator of their well-being.

Perceived importance of contributing to the community and society
Similarly, if we argue that children are contributing to society and not mere beneficiaries, then the acceptance of that notion is an indicator of child well-being.

Civic and Community Activities

In this subdomain, we turn from indicators of values and awareness to those that measure actual activity. In fact, we tried to compose our indicators in a complementary way. Thus, almost each indicator of values or awareness has a mirror indicator measuring the actual activity that results from the former. While doing so, we are enabled to collect data not only through self-reporting surveys, but also through various studies and through administrative data.

Percentage of children who belong and are active in a civic organization (political, community service, religious, or in general)
If, as mentioned, we believe it is important to be active on civic matters, then it would not be enough to only measure wherever our children think civic life is important. We would also need to measure the extent to which they are involved in such activities. We believe that such activity is part of general well-being. It contributes to the child's sense of self as well as to the society's civic health.

Such an indicator could be measured by using administrative data, such as archives of various organizations. It could also be measured by self-report surveys and by conducting special studies on children's time use or activities.

Percentage of children who report having political, religious, or social discussions with family and friends
Civic activity does not occur only in organizations; it also occurs in homes and social environments. Such involvement is an important component of children's well-being. Unfortunately, since this form of involvement cannot be measured through administrative data, we must rely on self-reports.

Percentage of children who volunteer
Finally, a special aspect of children's civic activity is volunteer activity. The literature supports the connection between volunteering and children's well-being (Torney-Purta, Schwille & Amadeo, 1999). Such a connection is also supported by the moral view of volunteering and children's well-being. This indicator could be measured both by administrative data and by studies and surveys.

Opportunities for Civic and Community Activities

Values, awareness, and even activities are not enough in themselves for studying children's well-being in relation to civic life skills. The opportunities a society offers children for such activities is a vital component of their well-being.

Those opportunities could be measured and analyzed by using administrative data. They can also be based on studies and surveys. A critical aspect of any such data collection would have to be the children's perspective on those opportunities and not just the adult view. After all, even if the opportunity exists, if the children do not know about it or perceive it as inaccessible to them, it would not really be an opportunity.

Percentage of children who are attending schools with student governments
Schools are the main settings where children spend their time. Schools are not a voluntary setting. Thus the mere fact of existence or nonexistence of student government could serve as a good indicator for children's opportunities to be involved in civic activities. We acknowledge the fact that the mere existence of a student government does not necessarily imply actual opportunities for child participation, but we think it is an essential step in the right direction and one that is simple to measure.

Degree of child participation in decision making about their lives
A more sophisticated level of opportunity for child participation can be measured by using this indicator. Such an indicator measures not only the existence of the mechanism for child participation, but also actual child participation. Child participation is well connected to child well-being and rights in various works and studies (Hodgkin & Newell, 1998; Melton & Limber, 1992; Melton & Saks, 1985). It is also well rooted in the concept of children's rights (Andrews & Kaufman, 1999).

This indicator could be measured at a number of different levels. At the societal level, a thorough examination of the legislation and children's legal standing in various institutions and procedures affecting their lives could be analyzed (Council of Europe, 1996; Melton & Saks, 1985). At a more institutionalized level, the degree to which children are entitled to participate in any decision concerning their lives in social institutions (schools, camps, boarding houses, etc.) could be assessed based on the institutions' bylaws or patterns of behavior. Finally, at an individual level, participation could be measured through surveys asking the children themselves about their perceived degree of participation.

Adult/government reaction[12] to children's participation
Opportunities alone are not enough. Moreover, in many cases they could be misleading. Even if the opportunities formally exist, the adult/government reaction is vital for making such opportunities meaningful. Thus, measuring this reaction is an important indicator for child well-being. It could be measured in two ways. First, a survey of government officials, teachers, caregivers, or just adults could provide important insights. A thorough analysis of case studies could serve as a complementary effort to elaborate this important indicator.

Opportunities for voluntary work of children
We have discussed previously the importance of voluntary work, which could be measured at two levels. The first uses organizational registry data to give us knowledge about possible places and opportunities for such work. The second would be based on asking the children their perception of the existence of opportunities for voluntary work.

---

[12] By reaction we refer to attitudes, perceptions and actions

Belief in one's ability to bring about change
Finally, the literature strongly supports the idea that a belief in the ability to change is almost a necessary condition for actually being able to participate in civic life. This last indicator in the domain may belong to the values and awareness subdomain, but it also has a clear connection to the opportunities subdomain. It is clear that the only way to measure this indicator would be through self-reports or individual testing of children.

PERSONAL LIFE SKILLS

We have already noted the importance of personal life skills to child well-being. In this domain, as in most of the others, in order to better deal with presenting specific indicators, we found it helpful to divide it into three subdomains-- interpersonal skills and resources, academic skills and resources, and intrapersonal skills and resources It is particularly worth noting that all of the indicators mentioned in this domain are especially age sensitive, and many are very much culturally contingent. Thus, we are suggesting the indicators for assessing the status of children, but the interpretation of the findings should be carefully done in accordance with the age group and the society/culture.

Interpersonal Skills and Resources

The literature about measures and indicators in this specific sub-domain is quite extensive. We have decided to focus on only on four indicators which we felt most comfortable with.

Support from family, friends and others
We know today, probably as we knew in the past, that child well-being is contingent on the existence of social support from various networks (Adler & Adler, 1998; Thompson, 1995). The literature is clear that the support of a significant adult is critical for healthy child development. We would like to emphasize the importance of such resources for the present well-being of children as well. Various scales have been developed to assess and measure the extent and quality of social networks. A number of them could be used in order to measure children's well-being. In our opinion, any scale that has been proven to be sound could be used, as long as the scale uses the child's perceptions and evaluation of the support and is not limited to the perspective of the adults concerned, and as long as it is used in a developmental way and rather than as a fixed concept (Morrow, 1999).

Conflict resolution skills

We previously dealt with the harmful consequences of adult violence toward children on children's well-being. It is evident that peer group violence and even participating in violence against others has equally dire consequences. This indicator is not only empirically grounded, but also ethically based. Accepting the notions of children's rights and human rights in general must lead to a conclusion that any conflict resolution that is not done in peaceful ways harms the well-being of children. A number of conflict-resolution scales exist and have been tested in the past (Straus & Donnelly, 1994; Straus & Gelles, 1990). Any of them, which have been validated, could be used to assess conflict-resolution skills.

Communication skills

If children are to become active and contributing members of society, the development and existence of communication skills is vital. Children start communicating their first days and continue to communicate through all ages. The ability to communicate is basic for a child's social life and well-being. Once again, a number of psychological scales and tests aimed at assessing communication skills at various ages exist. The source of information for this indicator would therefore be assessing samples of children in various age groups and then aggregating the data into an overall measure of children's well-being.

Behavior among and within peer groups

The significance and contribution of a child's peer group to his or her well-being has long been recognized (Adler & Adler, 1998). Patterns of child behavior among a group of peers and individuals provide a valuable insight into the child's world and well-being. Learning how children behave when they are without adult supervision will provide valuable insights into their lives and their well-being.

Although peer group behavior is a more "traditional" indicator, we propose to study it from a different perspective. We argue that the best source of information for studying child behavior patterns with peers would be "subjective" self-reports collected from the children themselves through surveys. We acknowledge that much has been learned and could still be learned by trying to secure "objective" observations of child behavior. Nevertheless, we believe that not only is there much to learn from the children, but also that their subjective reports will be more relevant for assessing their well-being.

Academic Skills and Resources

Many indicators exist in this field. A number of studies concentrated on school readiness and school achievements by children (Philip & Love, 1995). The OECD has started a special project of developing such indicators (Bottani, 1994), and studying school readiness has certainly become trendy in recent years. Nevertheless, we have decided to concentrate on only three indicators in this field, all of which should be studied with sensitivity to age and culture.

Literacy and numeracy level
This might be the most basic of all the educational indicators. In fact, it is already measured and monitored in many countries using various formal tests (see Chapter 2 for more details). Any test that has been proven to be sound can be used. However, one should be careful to use appropriate tests that would be culturally sensitive.

It is, however, worth noting that this indicator's importance has traditionally been contingent on a future-oriented focus. It has concentrated on how well our children are prepared for their next stage of life (either within childhood or in adulthood). We would like to add depth to this indicator by looking at it as a resource and an enabling factor for present well-being. We believe that since children are living in social contexts, their ability to perform within the skill range of their peers is an important aspect of their well-being.

Technological knowledge level
In a world that has entered a rapidly developing high- technology era, it is not enough for children's well-being to secure literacy and numeracy. Both from a future-oriented perspective and from a peer-comparison perspective, it is vital for a child's well-being that s/he achieve a high level of technological knowledge. A number of tests and scales already exist for this skill, although much fewer than for literacy and numeracy. Thus, there is still room for developing new tools for assessing technological knowledge.

Level of "general knowledge" (i.e.,, history, arts, geography, culture, etc.)
Finally, literacy, numeracy, and technological knowledge are not enough to secure children's well-being. Each and every culture has its own fundamental shared general knowledge. Usually, it would include the specific social history, traditions, and culture. If, as we believe, children's

well-being is contingent upon their participation in social life as contributors and not only as beneficiaries, then securing a minimum level of general knowledge would be necessary for well-being.

Since this suggested indicator is heavily culturally contingent, the only way it could be measured is by developing specific scales and tools for specific cultures and societies. These tools are yet to be developed. They would be heavily value contingent and thus the process of developing them would not be an isolated academic process.

Intrapersonal Skills and Resources

The previous two subdomains have focused on the relations between children and their environment. This last subdomain is focused directly on the child. Naturally it draws heavily on research findings in the fields of psychology and psychiatry.

Anxiety, depression, and general well-being
A number of scales and tests of well-being and its counterpoised anxiety and depression already exist and are in use. Much more attention, however, has been given to measuring and assessing anxiety and depression than to measuring well-being (Rettig & Leichtentritt, 1999; Terry & Huebner, 1995). In recent years, however, a number of attempts have been made to measure children's psychological well-being (Lyubomirsky & Lepper, 1999). Especially worth noting are the two scales (SLSS and MSLSS) developed by Huebner (Huebner, 1997; Huebner, Gilman & Laughlin, 1997).

Some of those efforts are proving to be valuable. We argue in favor of the scales that try to capture the positive end of children's psychological status rather than concentrating only on the negative aspects of their lives. Nevertheless, this field is still in its early stages and we cannot mark a specific or even a number of scales that should be used.

School behavior problems
One of the best outcome measures for children's intrapersonal well-being is their school behavior. By using both administrative data and surveys, we can learn about children's well-being through their school behavior. One should note, however, that the mere absence of school behavior problems is not enough to assure children's well-being. This negative indicator should be changed in the future to positive school behavior as a more valid indicator of

children's well-being. Unfortunately, there is not enough sound data yet to revise the indicator in that direction.

Perceived well-being

As a complementary aspect of the well-being indicator, we recommended that the child's perceived well-being and quality of life also be measured. We need to ask children in all age groups to evaluate their well-being. Such an effort could also serve as a part of assessing the "objective" well-being of children, but does not necessarily have to go along with it.

Self-perceived well-being can be gauged through the use of self-reported levels of happiness and satisfaction. Once again, by asking children in all age groups and cultures about their self-perception--how happy and satisfied they are--we believe we can learn much about their lives and gain much more knowledge about children's well-being (Huebner, 1994).

Perceived self-efficacy

Finally, we suggest that we use self-reports of children not only for learning how happy they are, but also for getting an insight into their self-efficacy. The literature indicates that a correlation exists between self-reports and actual self-efficacy as measured by various tests. It also supports the notion that often children know their situation much better than anybody else.

SAFETY AND PHYSICAL STATUS

Safety and physical status are commonly considered the most basic components of well-being. A child who is not safe will likely neither live nor develop in an optimal way and may also be more vulnerable to physical injury and trauma. Many studies have been done on the issue of children's health and safety. Naturally they come mainly from the disciplines of health, pediatrics, and public health. Many have also worked on perceptions of safety and the consequences of living in unsafe environments (Garbarino, 1995). Thus a broad base of knowledge exists in this domain. Once again we have decided to split it into two subdomains-- safety and physical status. We believe such a differentiation will clarify the content of the domain. However, it may be that physical status is a subset of safety.

Safety

Prevalence of child abuse and neglect in its various forms
During the last few decades, we have witnessed a growing awareness of the extent of violence against children in their homes, in institutions, and in the community. Along with the growing awareness of the prevalence of child abuse and neglect has come a growing understanding of the consequences of living in such conditions, both for child well-being and well-becoming. Undoubtedly, child abuse and neglect is seen and understood today as a major threat to the well-being of children.

This indicator, which is well grounded in research is a negative indicator – meaning that abolishing child abuse would not ensure safety or happiness. There are multiple sources of information for measuring this indicator. In many countries, a central registry has been established, thus enabling us to gather administrative data on abuse and neglect reports. In many other countries, surveys provide data from family members and the children themselves (Straus & Donnelly, 1994). Our experience leads us to conclude that using both sources will probably be the best option for measuring this indicator.

Prevalence of the use of corporal punishment of children
Recent investigation has shown that the negative implications of violence toward children do not stop at abuse and neglect (Straus & Donnelly, 1994). Furthermore, accepting the concept of children's rights and the fact that children are human beings eliminates any possible excuse for using corporal punishment against them. Just as violence is not an acceptable means for solving disputes between adults, it should not be used to solve disputes between adults and children (Hodgkin & Newell, 1998).

This indicator, we are suggesting, is better grounded in the way we see children and childhood and less in the existing knowledge, although some substantial knowledge on the issue has been gathered. The source of information for measuring this indicator should be through conducting surveys both among adults (parents) and children (Hauser, 1992; Straus & Donnelly, 1994).

Perception of safety among children from different age groups
Whereas the indicators just mentioned are trying to capture the extent to which physical acts take place, this indicator deals with perceptions. We

argue that it is important to measure perceptions of children and parents about children's safety. Numerous studies have shown the connection between perceptions of safety and the well-being of children. Thus, it is an indicator that is well grounded in theory and knowledge. Being a perception indicator, the only possible source of information would be surveys. We would like to emphasize here the need to ask children directly as much as the need to ask all children, especially from all age groups (Straus, 1999).

Exposure of children to environmental hazards
As we shift from the mere survival of children to their well-being, it is evident that we need to study and monitor the environment within which our children are living. The ecological approach to child well-being (Bronfenbrenner, 1979) has provided a valuable contribution for understanding the context of children's well-being (Andrews, 1997; Andrews & Ben-Arieh, 1999). Within this context, special concern has been placed on environmental hazards (Garbarino, 1995).

Once again we are dealing with a well-grounded indicator. It is certainly a "beyond-survival" indicator. The challenge, however, is that of operationalization and actual measurement. The ecological theory leads us to a situation where environmental hazards can be identified and analyzed at virtually any level (i.e.,,, from within the house to the diminishing rainforests). We suggest concentrating on the home and neighborhood levels. If so, there would be two possible sources of information. By using surveys we can ask children and their parents to identify hazards in their environment, and the prevalence and seriousness of these hazards could be used as an indicator. Similarly, by using administrative data on the type and scope of safe areas for children, we can measure the environmental hazards children are facing. Finally we can use administrative data on negative outcomes for children as it is elaborated in the next indicator.

Rate of hospital hospitalization due to trauma
This outcome indicator is recognized more and more as a vital one for studying the well-being of children beyond survival. Considered by many, as a "new" epidemic threatening child well-being, the rate of children who are injured or hurt either intentionally or unintentionally is an important indicator. It could be measured through surveys or through existing administrative data on children admitted to emergency room care or by the rate of hospitalization due to trauma. Other possibilities for using administrative data would be the school system data on injuries, insurance

companies' data and when available, and aggregate data on children using primary health care for the treatment of injuries.

Rate of child death by age and cause
This survival indicator, which is traditionally used around the world, continues to be of vital importance for studying children's well-being. This would especially be true if the focus would not be only on infant mortality or under-5 mortality rate, but rather on an attempt to include all cases of child morbidity and especially on analyzing morbidity rates by age and cause.

Physical Status

Substance (tobacco, alcohol and drugs) abuse by age
If children's injuries have a rival as the new epidemic disease of children in the industrialized world, then most certainly it would be substance abuse. Vast numbers of studies have all come to the same simple conclusion – substance abuse (and especially drug abuse and other illegal abuse) is directly harming children's well-being, and in most cases the abuse could either be prevented or treated (Ottomanelli, 1995; Rouse, 1995; Stoil & Hill, 1996).

Thus, the importance of this indicator is clear and sound. In fact, we can say that substance abuse is one of the most frequently used indicators, at least in the industrialized world. It is usually measured by surveys conducted among youth and their parents, but data also exist at an administrative level in archives of the police, the educational system, and presumably in hospitals and other health facilities.

Height, weight and body mass index measures
These beyond-survival measures are meant to monitor how well children develop physically. The health literature has been very progressive in suggesting development curves. Without underestimating the complexity of standards and measures of physical development particularly in relation to puberty, gender, and physical growth, i8t seems we could monitor children's well-being in comparison to such suggested curves. Such data could be collected through routine screening of children in various age groups, which could be placed in an administrative data archive for analyzing and comparisons over time.

Level and incidence of physical activity
Once again these indicators are well grounded in research establishing the importance of physical activity for children's well-being. It should be noted here that we deal with this indicator in more detail under the children's activities domain. Nevertheless, based on the health literature, we can assume a connection between physical activity and well-being, and hence the importance of this beyond-survival indicator. This indicator would be best measured through surveys among various age groups. It could be measured through time-use studies or could be assessed through health status screening of children or administrative data on their physical activity at school.

Eating habits and diet
Similar to the previous indicator, research has shown the connection between eating habits, diet, and children's well-being, Reasonable eating habits contribute both to the child's physical development and to her/his well-being. On one end of the continuum, lack of food or specific nutrients can lead to problems in physical development and children's well-being. On the other end, eating too much or having an unbalanced diet could also lead to physical disorders and consequences for emotional and general well-being.

As in the case of the previous indicator, we believe that this indicator would also be best measured through surveys among various age groups. It could also be assessed through health status screening gathered in an administrative data archive.

CONCLUSIONS

In this chapter we have suggested a list of some fifty indicators for children's well-being. These indicators are divided into five domains of children's well-being (as presented in Chapter 4), and further by a number of subdomains within each domain. It is our belief that the use of the complete list will result in much more complete knowledge of children's lives and a better understanding of their well-being and the forces that influence it.

The indicators that were suggested adhere to the basic approach and assumptions that were at the base of our project (see Chapter 3). Furthermore, they are based on a variety of sources of information. We have suggested indicators that can be studied using administrative data, analysis of the legislative status of children, and general social norms. Other indicators are based on time-use studies and various scales and tests. Finally, many of the indicators would have to draw on self-reporting surveys. It is important to reemphasize the need for asking children directly and for taking seriously their subjective knowledge or reports. In all cases, the unit of observation must be the child. Data could be collected from others in the family, community, or society, but we must look at children and take their perspective into account.

Finally, as much as we would like this list to be looked at as a comprehensive approach, we acknowledge that others might legitimately decide to select from among what we have suggested. This is certainly a possibility, which we can live with, as long as the guiding principles are respected.

CHAPTER 6

HOW TO MEASURE AND MONITOR CHILDREN'S WELL-BEING

The scope and innovative nature of the proposed domains and indicators of children's well-being are in many ways both reasons for hope and reasons for despair. When looking at the list of proposed indicators in the previous chapter, it seems the most vital aspect of their acceptance and use is the existence of data, or at least the possibility of identifying sources of information and an adequate way to collect the data.

The richness of children's lives and their domains of well-being lead to the conclusion that any single source of information will be inadequate. Any attempt to develop children's well-being indicators will have to be built on different types and sources of information. By and large, we refer to three major sources of information: administrative data, census and surveys, and primary (qualitative) research.

This chapter will discuss these sources, while trying to assess the advantages and disadvantages of each. We start by identifying the characteristics of each of the three sources of information. We then review the current use of each available source of data for measuring and monitoring children's well-being. Following the discussion of the current use, we point out challenges and limitations of using each data source. Even though the examples we provide in the chapter are primarily drawn from the experiences of only a few countries, we believe that the general concept can be easily applied to data gathering, and is applicable virtually everywhere. Based on the discussion of each of the three data sources, we suggest how measurements and indicators could be improved. Then we look into the limitations of descriptive indicators for children's well-being, and finally into the issue of indicators in context.

A. Ben-Arieh et al (eds.), Measuring and Monitoring Children's Well-Being, 91–105.
© 2001 *Kluwer Academic Publishers. Printed in the Netherlands.*

ADMINISTRATIVE DATA

Administrative data are data that are regularly and consistently collected in support of an organization's functions and stored within that organization's information system. Administrative databases are created primarily to monitor utilization, to determine the consumption of resources, and to ascertain the capacity to supply services (Dept. of Human Services, 1991). Although not collected primarily for research purposes, they are powerful resources for research and statistics (Goerge, 1997a; Goerge, 1997b).

Administrative data are an important source of information on the conditions of children. The data are maintained by organizations that serve children and families on a day-to-day basis, yet receive relatively little attention from researchers who are interested in monitoring child well-being. Until recently, administrative data would have been thought of as paper files rather than "data" to be used for research purposes. However, as these information systems become more computerized and accessible, administrative data can be a rich source of information for monitoring children's well-being in a society.

Characteristics of Administrative Data

Administrative data are culled from systems that have two basic functions. A particular system may stress one of these functions over the other. The first function is reporting for the purpose of accountability or reimbursement from an external or oversight agency. The second function is internal tracking of individuals or the services that they receive for the purpose of decision support and supporting other activities of the organization. The tracking function is what we think about when we refer to management information systems. Typically, the tracking system provides richer data, since external reporting in the human services is usually limited to eligibility of the individual for services. Tracking data assumes that one is interested in information that identifies the individual child served, the individuals/organizations providing the service, the services, and the characteristics of these three entities.

A particular administrative database typically covers the population receiving a particular service or resource, or those having a particular status. In many cases, data on all individuals who have ever been in the database are kept in the database or archived so that longitudinal information is available. For example, foster care data, when properly formatted and carefully analyzed, can provide a powerful set of indicators on how children's well-being is threatened within children's own families to the extent that the local or state government and the courts decide to remove the children from their homes.

Administrative data, by definition, will cover the population of individuals or families with a particular status or receiving a particular service. Data on their address, or some geographic data, are often available, thus, making possible the development of indicators at the regional or local level, or "small region monitoring" (Banister, 1994). Unlike national social surveys, which, because of cost, cannot have sampling frames that include every local region and in many cases have samples so small that even larger regional indicators cannot be calculated reliably, the population coverage in administrative data allows for regional and local indicators to be produced.

Unlike social surveys or census data collection, administrative data collection is carried out by a professional whose primary responsibility is not data collection. There are both advantages and disadvantages to data collected in this manner. Those collecting the data are often affected by the results of an analysis of the administrative data, depending on how many operational or policy decisions are based on that information (Leginski et al., 1989). There are also issues (e.g.,, worker's use of time or confidentiality) other than optimal data collection that affect the data collection. Data collection can vary over time because of changes in operations or agency mandates. Finally, workers may take shortcuts or not provide certain data if they determine that certain data are not actually used in the operation of the agency.

On the positive side, these workers may have an interest in the quality of the data they collect if they actually use the data for their own decision making (Banister, 1994; Mugford, Banfield, & O'Hanlon, 1991). It is a commonly held assumption in information systems development that the more the data are used, the better that data will be. For data items that are necessary or mandatory to complete administration functions, the amount of missing data are likely to be minimal. There may be considerable access to the subjects so that incorrect data are more likely to be corrected than in social surveys or census data. Also, because the data are collected within the normal conduct of business, there is no interviewer inserted into the process to disrupt the lives of those studied, or to bias responses. This may be particularly important where data collection is around child abuse and neglect or mental health, or when it is difficult for an interviewer to be present during critical events.

The types of indicators one can most easily extract from administrative data are very much focused on problem-related outcomes and those events that should not happen (Iezzoni, 1990). Although the following questions focus on problems, they can also be turned around to state indicators in positive ways. What percentage of children are born without their mothers having received prenatal care? How many infants die within the first months of their lives? How many children are included in income assistance grants? How many children are removed from the custody of their parents? This negative focus seems obvious since the data are collected in the course of service provision intended to ameliorate problems.

One would expect that as computers become more a part of everyday life, there would be more data available on the non-risk aspects of children's lives. For example, as library systems become computerized, knowing how many children use libraries and borrow books can provide more information on normative aspects of children's lives. School performance data already provide such data on the educational achievement. Even in these examples, however, one can understand how the problem orientation is not necessarily in the data itself, but in how the data are analyzed.

A major limitation of administrative data is the fact that the data only include individuals and families who have entered the service system. This means that although administrative data are an excellent source of information for service users, the data do not provide any information on nonusers. In other words, the data only describe clients, not the overall population. Not having good information on the overall population will greatly reduce researchers' ability to study "population participation rates" or "incidence and prevalence rates." However, recent developments in geocoding technology, coupled with the availability of census population data at the level of a very small geographic unit, can solve some of these problems. Specifically, by using geocodes from the client addresses contained in administrative data with census tract data, we will be able to calculate prevalence or incidence rates of service use for particular subgroups of clients. This type of analysis has been shown to be a very useful method to study population incidence rates of rare events such as foster care placements (Goerge, Wulczyn, & Harden, 1994).

While discussing administrative data, attention should be given to the technical issues of data reliability, validity, and accuracy. Unfortunately, this may only be possible after the data have been analyzed. Although it is sometimes possible to take administrative data and do multistate or cross-country comparisons, the usefulness of such efforts might be limited if the exact identification of data categories is not comparable from one state or country to the next and because complete data sets are not available in all locations (Larson, Doris, & Alvarez, 1990; Masson & Gibbs, 1992).

To sum up, one can say that administrative data are an important information source that has not yet been used to full potential. Administrative data may be the best option for quickly developing more, timely, or new community and local indicators on children's well-being. Given the data collection expense of new or continuing social surveys, and given that much administrative data already exist, this source is ideal for the short-term development of indicators that can be used to inform the public and policy makers.

Some Examples for Using Administrative Data

One of the best examples of the use of administrative data to establish child well-being indicators is the United States vital statistics data--mostly data on births and deaths. Although these data are collected primarily for statistical purposes, each set of data has a clear set of administrative purposes. Many events are triggered or made possible by the fact that a birth or death certificate is issued--essentially anything that requires proof of birth or death. These two sets of data form a cornerstone of the state and federal health statistics in the United States; from these two databases, the number of births, teenage births, births to unmarried mothers, and causes of adolescent death, to name just a few, can be identified (Goerge, 1997).

Birth and death certificate data provide an example of how indicators can be developed by combining datasets. When birth certificates and death certificates are linked, it is possible, for example, to calculate infant mortality statistics. The importance and value of linking databases is crucial for developing new indicators and increasing the validity and accuracy of current indicators. However, linking records is often not possible with survey or Census Bureau data because of a lack of identifying information about individuals, or because of a lack of access due to confidentiality restrictions (Goerge, 1997).

There are a number of national indicators developed by the U.S. government from administrative data. These include information from public health statistics and many of the programmatic indicators in the "Green" book. The "Green" book, produced by the U.S. House Ways and Means Committee, is a compendium of statistics that makes the most of the results of analyses of administrative data, including AFDC (cash income maintenance), child welfare, and Supplemental Security Income, among others. In many cases, survey results enhance the analyses of administrative data (provided to the federal government by states), but more and better indicators are very much needed in many areas, including child care and child support enforcement. The development of tracking systems for child care and child support, which have already being established in many states, represent a step in that direction. The National Center for Health Statistics, most likely the best human service example of federal use of administrative data, uses vital statistics data from states to provide an extensive set of birth, death, and population indicators (e.g.,, Monthly Vital Statistics Reports). They also use the National Hospital Discharge Survey, which is based on a sample of administrative data on hospital discharges, that could be expanded with today's technology to include the entire population of children who are hospitalized.

The Kids Count project of the Annie E. Casey Foundation (see Chapter 2 for details) provides profiles of the condition of children in each of the states in the United States. Profiles include child health, adolescent births, juvenile crime, teen unemployment and school dropout, poverty, and household structure. These reports rely on analyses of administrative data focusing on yearly changes at the state level. Vital statistics and uniform crime reports are a key to developing the comparative indicators in the Kids Count reports.

CENSUS AND SURVEY DATA

Many of the recent efforts to monitor the well-being of children are based on census and other representative sample surveys, which are important sources of existing data. Indicators developed from census and survey data are being used increasingly as important tools for measuring and monitoring the well-being of children. However, there are limits to the usefulness of census and survey data--not only due to the nature of the data gathered, but also to how the data are currently used to construct various indicators (Lee, 1997).

Characteristics of survey data

Survey data in general are collected for pursuing specific research questions and therefore establish a clear definition of the population for the study. Researchers play a significant role in defining the population of interest for the sampling frame and designing survey instruments and protocols even before the data are collected. One advantage of survey data, then, are that by including relevant survey items the instruments, an in-depth inquiry of a particular area of interest is made possible. For example, the National Health

Interview Survey in the U.S. is specifically designed to collect in-depth data on health measures while the Survey of Income and Program Participation is designed to collect economic measures. Although targeted, in-depth information on selected subject areas is a major advantage of survey data collection, one significant drawback to using surveys is their significant expense.

Although many childhood indicators can be developed from the existing census and national survey data, there are limits to their usefulness. From the point of view of children's well-being, one drawback to such data is the fact that they collect only general information on the socioeconomic status of households and do not obtain sufficient information on children's activities or behaviors at the level of the individual child. Typically most income-related surveys collect the data at the household level and do not collect information on the distribution of financial resources among the household members.

A second drawback is that most surveys define the adult population as the target respondents. Even when the information is collected for child well-being studies, the information is normally collected by asking adult respondents; thus the information is "filtered" through the adult respondents' perceptions, rather than being collected first hand from the children themselves.

Some Examples of Census and Survey Data

For many of the recent efforts to monitor the well-being of children, the official periodic country census or other nationally representative sample surveys have been important sources of existing data.

For example, indicators of basic child characteristics including race/ethnicity, the number of children, and family structure and living arrangements are available from the decennial census and the National Survey of Children (NSC) in the United States. Data on the lives of children and their families, including family structure, families' annual income, parents' employment status, parents' education level, and the receipt of such cash and non-cash benefits are collected in Israel through the annual survey of households' income.

Measures related to general child health are collected annually in the National Health Interview Survey (NHIS) in the United States and every 5 years by the HBSC study in twenty-seven countries (see Chapter 2 for more details). Educational achievement and related behavior indicators are collected in the United States by the National Assessment of Educational Progress (NAEP), the National Household Education Survey (NHES), and the School Enrollment Supplement to the Current Population Survey (CPS). By and large, these data and measures have been developed to better understand the impact of changes in children's policies and shifts in sociodemographic trends on the well-being of children (Zill, Sigal, & Brim, 1982).

PRIMARY RESEARCH

We find it useful to distinguish primary research from social census and surveys (the methods of research dealt with previously). When referring to primary research we would like to emphasize especially the qualitative research within this category; however, we must note that primary research could include also quantitative research, which will still be differentiated from the census and surveys methods.

The main difference is that census and surveys are focused on collecting quantitative data on representative samples, while primary research, as we define it, looks at individuals or groups of children–but not necessarily on samples. Another distinction is the method used to gather data. Whereas census and survey data are based on asking a series of questions, primary research might use other methods of gathering data like observations, time-use diaries, and individual tests.

Characteristics of primary research

Primary research in general is conducted as a means of enriching our knowledge base. Its main purpose, as Furstenberg suggests, is to conduct research explicitly aimed at addressing the identified questions and gaps in knowledge (Furstenberg, 1997; Furstenberg & Huges, 1997). Primary research is expected to contribute to a better understanding of changes in family structure and the child's place in the family (Frones, 1997).

It seems apparent that our knowledge about children is not sufficient (Ben-Arieh, 1997; Furstenberg, 1997; Furstenberg & Huges, 1997; Jensen & Saporiti, 1992). Thus, the big challenge of conducting primary research is to enrich existing knowledge. This enriched knowledge should be used to plan better census and survey efforts as well as to make better use of administrative data. However, primary research and especially qualitative primary research should be used also directly for measuring and monitoring children's well-being.

Conducting qualitative research is immensely important for direct measurement and understanding of the well-being of children. Qualitative primary research is one of the best tools for measuring the subjective well-being of children. Qualitative primary research will enrich the existing knowledge base and provide better insight into the subjective well-being of children. Even more, using primary research would contribute to measuring and monitoring children's everyday activities and increase our understanding of children's well-being. Such research could contribute to a better understanding and monitoring of individual achievements. Finally, primary (qualitative) research would contribute to efforts to measure and monitor children's well-being from a developmental perspective, and will improve our understanding of subjective child well-being and subjective childhood experiences.

A major drawback of primary research as a source of information is the inability to generalize about the data gathered beyond the particular child population on which it is collected. Also a major outlay of resources is needed to conduct studies on a large scale and on a longitudinal basis.

Some Examples of Using Primary and Qualitative Research Data

As discussed previously, primary research data are collected mainly for the enrichment of knowledge that potentially can improve the design, collection, and understanding of administrative data and census and survey data. We argue that primary (qualitative) research data could also be used for direct measurement and monitoring of children's well-being.

First and foremost we would like to emphasize the value of time-use diaries and studies to measure and monitor children's well-being (see, for example, Plewis, Creeser, & Mooney, 1990). Other examples could be drawn from similar studies conducted for adults. A number of countries have conducted time-use diary studies periodically, but almost exclusively among adults.Another example is anthropological studies that focus on a group of children, following them for a period of time. Finally, documenting children's experiences and stories has also been done, but not widely enough for measuring and monitoring children's well-being (Tardieu, 1997).

DEVELOPING BETTER INDICATORS

Because most national surveys provide only general socioeconomic data, one challenge for effective and meaningful measuring and monitoring efforts is to expand the collection of information into other dimensions of childhood, such as children's daily activities. One good example of such an effort is the National Survey of America's Families (NSAF) that began its data collection in 1997. The NSAF is a major new survey based on a sampling frame that is representative of the nation as a whole, with a larger sample of thirteen individual states. The survey not only collects extensive information about the economic well-being of families, but also collects measures such as child school engagement, child behavioral and emotional problems, child cognitive stimulation, and children's activities.

Further, time-use studies of children, similar to those already conducted for adults, would be of great assistance. Such studies would enable us to describe the shape and form of children's daily activities, and would also allow comparison across countries, which vary in economic situation, culture, social organization, and policies towards children.

A potential strategy for better utilizing administrative data and improving indicators would be to combine administrative databases or administrative databases and survey or census data. By mixing and matching fields from numerous databases, it would be possible to increase the validity and accuracy of indicators. Perhaps most important, linking administrative data over years would provide a better time-series and offer the possibility of tracking outcomes longitudinally (Goerge, Wulczyn, & Harden, 1994; Hunter, 1994). Longitudinal data, combined with knowledge of policy and practice, would allow, at a minimum, analysis of relative child well-being over time.

Combining data from multiple sources also begins to allow investigators to study issues of service overlap for children and families who have multiple problems. The question of whether most (~80%) of the resources are going to a few (~20%) of the families or children (the "80/20" question) is important for welfare policies and human service management. Also, knowing how many children are poor and victims of abuse or neglect, or are poor and disabled, would provide those interested in improving the lives of children better information for developing policies and service programs.

There has also recently been more discussion of doing an administrative census that would combine various types of administrative data including AFDC and other income maintenance, income tax returns, and Social

Security data to provide an alternative to the current method of data collection (in the U.S.) for the decennial census. Such an effort could provide better information on some issues--data between census, for example--and would also provide a base population (the denominator) and measurement system to yield better prevalence and incidence rates of the host of indicators discussed in Chapter 5.

For example, in reviewing the 1990 census figures on minority infants with birth certificate data, a tremendous undercount in that subgroup was found (Goerge, Lee, Sommer, & Van Voorhis, 1993) when the impossible observation was made that over 100 percent of infants in Chicago were part of AFDC grants. It appears that, despite the adjustments made by the Census Bureau, the census undercounted the number of African American infants under 1 year of age living in Chicago. In order to calculate a more accurate figure, vital statistics data on the number of live African American births in Chicago from June 1989 to June 1990 was used after subtracting the number of infant deaths over the same period. For this type of information, an administrative census provided more accurate statistics (Goerge et al., 1993).

In order to do better small-region monitoring of child indicators, increased use of geocoding (address-matching) to allow for the aggregation of records at any geographic level is very important. If addresses exist in the database, they can be geocoded and any level of spatial aggregation is then possible. Individual-level data can be aggregated into census blocks and tracts and community or neighborhood areas. Geographic information also provides an additional piece of information for linking an individual's records across multiple databases.

LIMITATIONS OF DESCRIPTIVE CHILDHOOD SOCIAL INDICATORS

Although indicators of children's well-being have been used increasingly more often as important tools for measuring and monitoring the well-being of children, their usefulness is limited because most indicators are simple statistical descriptions of the conditions of children at the aggregate level. This limitation is not only due to the nature of the data gathered, but also to how the data are currently used to construct various indicators. In this section, we focus on two major limitations of the current children's well-being indicators: heavy reliance on descriptive indicators of the condition of children without sufficient modeling efforts; and use of highly aggregated data.

In order for such indicators to be useful, they should make it possible to assess the extent to which children's lives are being improved by social programs and policies. For instance, we ultimately want to find out how changes in such input indicators as family structure, family size, parental education and employment, family income, and changes in income maintenance programs are related to changes in such outcome indicators as measures of children's achievement, health, and behavior. Without an effort to relate indicator variables to one another, at both micro and macro levels, and to test why specific changes in outcome indicators are occurring using systematic indicator models, it would be impossible to disentangle the effects of various input indicators and to estimate the "true" effect of policies and program changes on child well-being indicators. As discussed by Testa, it is essential to build a conceptual model that identifies the likely influences that impinge on specific measures of child well-being in order to be able to use the indicators to guide social policies (Testa, 1990).

Another limitation of most previous children's well-being indicators results from the use of highly aggregated data. Much of the past literature on childhood indicators research used aggregate data focusing on the relationship between macro-level dependent variables (for example, rates of child poverty) and group-level independent variables (e.g.,, area racial/ethnic composition, proportion of single-parent families). One major concern has been whether inferences about the behavior of individuals can be made on the basis of an analysis that uses aggregate data. Aggregate data often obscure the relationship of interest by suppressing variations in the variables across individuals by aggregating across individuals. Hypothetical data on poverty and family structure are presented in Table 1 to illustrate how an analysis at the aggregate level can be problematic in making inferences about the relationship of interest at the individual level. Table 1 presents the prevalence of poverty and single-parent households in hypothetical communities A and B.

TABLE 2. HYPOTHETICAL DATA ON HOUSEHOLD TYPE AND POVERTY

	Community A				Community B		
	Poor	Not Poor	Total		Poor	Not Poor	Total
Single Parent	20	40	60	Single Parent	5	25	30
Two Parent	30	10	40	Two Parent	15	55	70
Total	50	50	100	Total	20	80	100

Each community has 100 households. In community A, single parents head 60 percent of the households and 50 percent of the households are poor. In community B, on the other hand, single parents head 30 percent and 20 percent are poor. By examining the relationship between single parenthood and poverty using the aggregate community data, one would conclude that single-parent households are more likely to be poor because a higher percentage of single-parent households in a community is related to a higher percentage of households being poor. However, disaggregated data by poverty status and single parenthood reveal a completely different picture. In community A, 33 percent (20/60) of single-parent households are poor in comparison to 75 percent (30/40) of two-parent households in poverty. Also, in community B, 16 percent (5/30) of single-parent households are poor compared to 21 percent (15/70) of two-parent households. In fact, in both communities A and B, single-parent households are *less* likely to be in poverty in the hypothetical data presented in Table 1. (One would find similar results combining disaggregated data from community A and B.) As shown in this example, using aggregate-level data (in this case, community poverty rates and single parenthood rates) to make inferences about the relationship at the individual unit (in the example, the relationship between poverty and household structure at the household level) becomes quite problematic.

MEASURING THE STATE OF THE CHILD: A CONTEXTUAL PERSPECTIVE

Understanding the impact of social structure and policies or programs on individual child well-being has long been an important subject in the field of children's well-being indicators. In this section, we suggest that individual well-being is influenced not only by the child's attributes, but also by the characteristics of the contextual factors that include policy interventions as well as the characteristics of the family and neighborhood. If we are to enhance our ability to measure the conditions of children, we must improve our strategies for measuring both the conditions of individual children and families and the contextual-level ecology in which they are embedded. It will require a conceptual model that integrates individual, family, and contextual-level factors.

A *contextual* perspective regarding human development emphasizes the significance of interactions among the individual, family, peer group, activity setting (such as schools and day care centers), residential neighborhood, the broader community, and society at large (Bronfenbrenner, 1979). The term "context" typically refers to a social unit that shares space, patterned interaction, collective perception of boundaries and identity, and shared feelings of belonging. Individuals tend to relate to several contexts, such as their residential neighborhood, work place, religious congregation, and geographic region of their family's origin.

The structure and processes of such contexts are believed to facilitate or hinder access to social and material resources necessary for a child's survival, development, protection, and participation. Beneficial resources must be available close to where the young people spend their time in their homes, schools, and other activity settings. The young people and their caregivers must be able to access and use the resources. Family resources include financial assets, time for social interaction, and such human capital as parental education, skills, and mental health. Community resources include aspects of the physical, economic, and social environment that create productive and healthy opportunities for individuals and families.

These family and community contextual variables create an environment that offers constraints and/or opportunities for children while they are growing up. These sets of contextual forces, along with the individual child's attributes, affect the child's developmental outcomes. Thus, because of the complexity of measuring children's well-being, a model that integrates individual, family, and contextual-level factors is required. In other words, the individual child's well-being is influenced not only by micro-level attributes but also by the macro-level contextual variables.

For the purpose of guiding children's policies, it is very important to build an analytical dimension that is based on a conceptual framework of interrelating micro- and macro-factors to the childhood social indicators work. For example, understanding variations in descriptive childhood indicators, such as child poverty rates, often requires the deconstruction of descriptive patterns or trends into those constituent changes due shifts in macro sociodemographic characteristics (e.g.,, changes in racial composition in a neighborhood, changes in area employment rates, outmigration of the population); any policy or program changes in related areas (e.g.,, higher/lower income maintenance reimbursement rates); and changes in individual characteristics (e.g.,, changes in a child's living arrangement or parental employment status).

Most previous childhood social indicators research has failed to address the "micro-macro" relationships that are essential to understanding the social and demographic causes of changing trends in children's well-being. In recent years, however, there has been growing interest among researchers in conceptualizing and measuring contextual effects. For example, using community disorganization theory, Sampson found that the impact of community is found primarily in the factors that facilitate or inhibit networks of social support. Controlling for individual differences, mothers in areas characterized by social isolation, sparse networks, and weak social supports are more apt to abuse their children. He concludes that

> the nexus of child abuse, infant mortality, low birth
> weight, and other child health problems is engendered
> by structural and cultural community disorganization
> (Sampson, 1993).

Other studies using a social ecological model, have also found support for the concept of neighborhood risk, that is, the notion that the same family is more likely to have poorer outcomes in one neighborhood than in another (Garbarino, 1995).

CONCLUSIONS

In this chapter, we briefly outlined the three major sources of data on child well-being indicators and offered advantages and disadvantages of each. It is our view that gaining a better understanding of children's well-being requires mixing and matching different data sources and methods. Relying on any single source of information will always be a limited way to construct the complete picture of child well-being. Thus, the task of compiling the child well-being indicators we outline in this book calls for a close collaboration of practitioners and researchers using a variety of methods.

We need to move beyond simple descriptive measures of highly aggregated child well-being indicators--especially if the ultimate use of these indicators is to affect national, regional, and local policies. To achieve improved outcomes for children, we must improve our strategies for measuring the conditions of individual children and also the contextual-level ecology in which they are embedded.

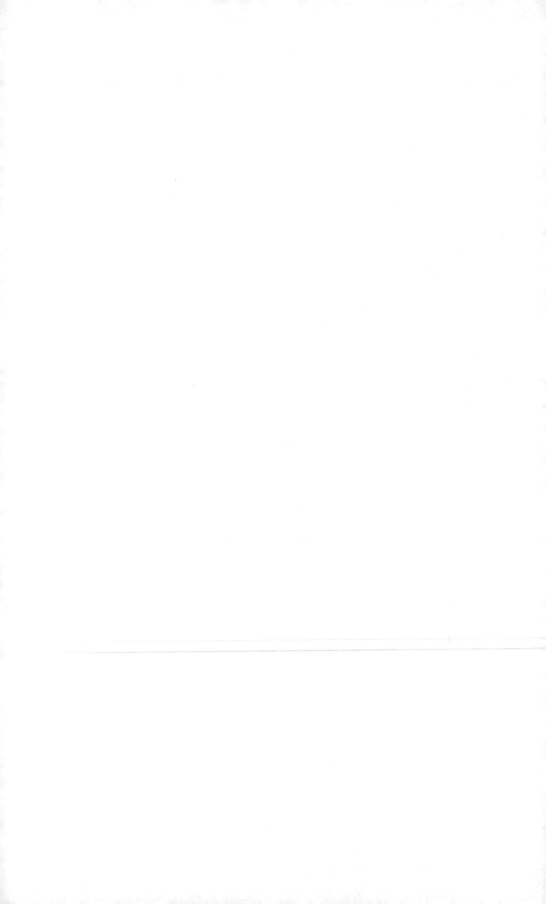

CHAPTER 7

MEASURING AND MONITORING CHILDREN'S WELL-BEING AT THE COMMUNITY LEVEL

A strong community is one in which children and youth are physically and emotionally healthy and safe, are able to learn according to their potential, and are demonstrating age-appropriate personal skills and responsibility by participating in social, economic, and civic life. In democratic societies, people of all ages, young and old, can and often do organize in their neighborhoods and communities to promote children's well-being.

Any effort to assess and promote children's well-being must be community-based, because that is where children and their families live. Compilation of information at regional, state, and national levels are useful for policy purposes, as discussed in the next chapter. But the more aggregated one's data, the more one is forced to rely on measures of central tendencies, and the unique variations in particular populations and communities are lost. Thus particular strengths and vulnerabilities of children in atypical circumstances may be overlooked.

The assessment of children's well-being is only one part of the equation – literally, the state of children is about their conditions and lives. If positive change is to be promoted, a community must also assess resources available to children. This requires assessing information about the environmental context of the child, including such factors as immediate and extended family characteristics, social networks, concrete resources such as food, water, housing, or transportation, and community institutions such as schools, recreational resources, and work opportunities (Andrews, 1997; Hancock, 1999).

COMMUNITY ORGANIZING FOR CHILD WELL-BEING

In the wake of widespread efforts to promote comprehensive community planning and action for well-being across the life span, many local governments and nongovernmental organizations (NGOs) have developed specific child and youth councils that are essentially charged with promoting

107

A. Ben-Arieh et al (eds.), Measuring and Monitoring Children's Well-Being, 107–117.
© 2001 Kluwer Academic Publishers. Printed in the Netherlands.

child well-being. These comprehensive efforts include such programs as the Coalition for Healthier Cities and Communities (Annie E. Casey Foundation, 1999) and youth-focused initiatives inspired by programs like the Annie E. Casey Foundation "Kids Count" initiative in the U.S.(see chapter 2 for details) and the Search Institute (Andress & Roehlkepartain, 1993).

Measuring and monitoring the status of children is a crucial component in any community action process. The University of Kansas "Community Tool Box" program, refers to *community capacity* as the ability of community members to make a difference over time and across different issues (Nagy, 1999). Measuring and monitoring children's well-being could provide information for on-going needs, resource assessment and evaluation efforts that are part of any such process. To maximize the chances of success the following steps would be essential (Berkowitz, 1999; Kretzmann & McKnight, 1993; Mondross & Wilson, 1994; Samuels, Ahsan, & Garcia, 1995):

1. Organizing and sustaining community action groups that are inclusive of representatives of all groups affected by the issues of concern;

2. Developing and sustaining supportive partnerships with all sectors of the community;

3. Conducting comprehensive needs and resource assessments pertinent to the focus issue;

4. Analyzing, interpreting, and attaining consensus about the meaning of the assessments;

5. Exploring alternative courses of action to address the issues for positive change;

6. Choosing a collective course of action;

7. Implementing the action;

8. Evaluating the action;

9. Re-assessing needs and resources; and

10. Sustaining the planning – action cycle.

The use of information gained from measuring and monitoring the well-being of children generally occurs during the needs and resource assessment and evaluation processes. A typical community planning process will include a needs and resource assessment around broad or focused topics, asset assessment, geographic mapping of the data, and ethnographic or qualitative data (e.g., photos, and situational or population anecdotes). Most assessments use a combination of administrative data, census and survey data and primary research data collection (see Chapter 6 for more details).

Often the studies are cross-sectional; that is, they are like a snapshot in time, with no plan for repeated measures or trend analysis or monitoring. A thorough effort to measure and especially to monitor children's well-being (as in the community benchmarking processes) will prove to be especially helpful because they anticipate data collection and analysis over time.

Communities vary in their capacities to collect data and to use it for promoting children's well-being. Clearly, those that are based in technologically rich areas with highly educated populations are at an advantage in terms of the amount and detail of recorded data. Although disparities in access to information technology across communities, cultures, and societies are vast, all but the most disorganized areas have some level of information system. In any setting, an investment in measuring and monitoring children's well-being is both essential and fruitful, especially if used to include leadership, data personnel, facilitators to promote participation in providing and interpreting data, and a willing group of activists or policymakers who will use the information to stimulate change.

MEASURING CHILDREN'S WELL-BEING AT THE COMMUNITY LEVEL

Whether the information is gathered through sophisticated statistical methods, administrative data, focus groups rich oral participation, or a combination of methods, the measurement process must attend to a number of factors in order to promote its effectiveness in communities. Those factors include, inclusivity and cultural relevance, reliability and validity, feasibility, repetition, facilitation of interpretation, and utility.

Inclusivity and cultural relevance
Inclusion poses one of the more challenging aspects of community planning. In the case of children and youth, all sectors of a community should be represented in the decision making process about the target population, the

data collection, and the community planning and action. This requires developing group processes and data collection methods that are relevant within and across class, ethnicity, race, age, gender, ability, and other aspects of a diverse society.

Reliability and validity
In the next chapter we summarizes several criteria for indicators of children's well-being. At the community level one should be aware that indicators of children's well-being need to have meaning in that level by being relevant and to the purpose of the community action group and understandable to the group. Information must be appropriately generalizable and meet standards of reliability and internal and external validity.

Feasibility
Community groups with vision and creativity can generate numerous ideas about helpful information, but constraints of instrumentation, cost, time, complexity, and other factors may make collection of such information unrealistic. Often groups must settle for less than ideal indicators because they are feasible to collect.

Repetition
Assuming pilot studies indicate that the chosen measures are a true representation of the status of children in the community, they should be collected within the context of a plan for monitoring the indicators over time through repeated measurement. Such a plan requires a sustained planning commitment and investment of future resources. The repetition need not occur every year; multi-year cycles are less expensive and yield useful information.

Facilitating the interpretation of information is also critical. Quantifiable and qualitative data are media through which community dialogues can be facilitated. Measures should be chosen with anticipation that they will contribute meaningfully to the discourse and potentially help guide decisions about action.

Utility

Information may have value in and of itself, but generally its value is in its utility. As measures are chosen, the various audiences (stakeholders) and potential uses of the data should be specified. Data are often collected for a specific group or purpose, but may have broader applications as well. For example, a community children's council may commission a monitoring study, but the area school districts or housing planning council may find it useful as well. Planning to get extensive use from a measuring and monitoring effort represents efficient use of resources.

HYPOTHETICAL COMMUNITY MEASURING AND MONITORING PROCESS

A hypothetical case example that compares two communities illustrates the utility of our suggested "new" domains and indicators, and provides a foundation for guiding communities in the use of the data for planning and action purposes. The results of the study are summarized in Table 3. The case is based on the following assumptions:

- The data in this table are one part of a more comprehensive study;
- A representative sample of children and parents/caregivers was included; efforts were made to include traditionally excluded populations (e.g.,, those who are institutionalized, in contained programs for children with disabilities, or homeless);
- Data was collected using a variety of methods, including valid, reliable, and culturally relevant surveys as well as qualitative methods, such as focus groups;
- In addition to descriptive summaries and measures of central tendency, analyses and commentary were presented to describe variations and attention to outliers or respondents in the statistical minority;
- Data are available by subpopulation (i.e.,, gender, racial/ethnic groups);
- Children between the ages of 10 and 13 and their parents / caregivers were involved in the design of the data collection methods, gathering data, and analysis of results;
- The primary users of the information are the members of the children and youth council, who are authorized to make planning and resource allocation decisions about resources for children and their families, although other groups in the community have also demonstrated keen interest in the studies;

- The data are collected every two years, trend analyses conducted, and interpretive reports prepared to explain positive and negative directions. On the table, note that the positive or negative trend indicators pertain to the value according to community opinion placed on the direction of the change, not the absolute change. For example, an increase in the percentage of children who use violence is regarded as a negative trend; a decrease in the percentage of children having sex without contraception is a positive trend.

Table 3. Hypothetical Community Data on the Well-being of Children Ages 10-13[13]

WELL-BEING INDICATOR	Percentage of All Children in the Community or Average Response / Trend[14]		Level Of Data [15]
	Smithville	Jonesville	
SAMPLE TRADITIONAL INDICATORS			
Family status			
Children 10-13 who live in homes with no adult male	29% -	58% -	F
Families with children age 10-13 with annual income below poverty	15% +	27% +	F
Education			
Parents (of children age 10-13) who completed high school	94% +	87% +	F
Children who failed their grade level	3% +	4% -	C
Risk behaviors			
Children who have used drugs more than twice	10% +	12% +	C
Children who report sexual activity without contraception	7% -	6% +	C
Children charged with violent offense at school or in community	12% +	15% +	C
SAMPLE NEW INDICATORS			
Safety and Physical Status			
Children who report feeling safe "most" or "all" of the time	49% -	33% +	C

[13] All figures are for children 10-13 unless otherwise specified,

[14] Community opinion regarding value of trend over past six years: + = positive trend - = negative trend

[15] C = Child level data; F = Caregiver, parent, or family level data; E = Ecological context level data

Table 3. Hypothetical Community Data on the Well-being of Children Ages 10-13 (continued)

WELL-BEING INDICATOR	Percentage of All Children in the Community or Average Response / Trend		Level Of Data
	Smithville	Jonesville	
Children who report "easy" access to exercise areas or facilities	38% +	45% +	E
Personal life skills			
Child's perceived social support from family is in "high" range	22% -	32% +	F
Child reports "moderately high" or "high" level of life satisfaction	33% -	38% -	C
Child reports "easy" access to professional help for coping with hard time	12% +	20% +	E
Civic life skills			
Average number of hours per week in community service	0.75 +	1.3 +	C
Within the community, available volunteer placements per child	0.1 +	0.3 +	E
Children's Activities			
Average number of hours per weekday in school, after-school tutoring, or doing homework	10.1 -	8.2 +	C
Average number of hours per day children spend in casual social interaction (direct contact, by phone or computer) with: Peers	0.4 -	2.1 +	C
Adults	0.2 -	0.1 -	C
Percentage of children who respond "Just about right" when asked, "The amount of time in a day when I can choose whatever I want to do is...."	3% -	20% -	C
Percentage of children who respond "confident" or "very confident" when asked to assess their confidence in their ability to do something musical, dramatic, artistic, or athletic	24% -	38% +	C
Percentage of parents who report the amount of time they spend with their child each day is "just about right"	32% -	24% -	F

Table 3. Hypothetical Community Data on the Well-being of Children Ages 10-13
(continued)

WELL-BEING INDICATOR	Percentage of All Children in the Community or Average Response / Trend		Level Of Data
	Smithville	Jonesville	
Percentage of children who report they have adequate access to places in their community where they can "hang out" with their friends	19% -	54% +	E
Economic conditions			
Percentage of children who have a means to earn income	48% -	46% -	C
For children who do paid work, average number of hours worked per week	3.5 +	1.5 +	C
Average amount of money spent at the child's discretion each week	$12.33 +	$8.24 +	C
Percentage of children who have participated in economic life skills programs that teach them how to get and keep a youth job	14% +	17% -	E

For this hypothetical example, let us assume the following sample themes were among those noted in the qualitative data:

- The time children spend interacting with adults is in fragmented bits of time spread across a day, and rarely involves extended conversation or participation in mutual activities;
- The type of paid work performed by children this age tends to be performing tasks in support of adults, e.g.,, yard work, delivering packages, babysitting;
- The places where children have access to exercise tend to be unsupervised multi-purpose public spaces, such as parks and undeveloped land.

Given the various caveats that the data in Table 1 are part of a greater study with richer qualitative data, the primary issue remains: *What is a community to DO with this information?*

With traditional indicators, the inclination is for community groups to express concern about the negative social signs and promote action to stop the negative trends: to stop drug use, school failure, children's isolation. Yet to monitor the indicator over time does not suggest what the children ARE doing. For example, if drug use and school failure rates go down, does that mean children are necessarily better off? The absence of a negative condition does not indicate the presence of a positive condition.

A critical principle in the use of community needs and resource assessments is that groups should hesitate to jump to solutions (Berkowitz, 1999). Careful analysis and interpretation of the data through extended discussion about the data and the possible reasons behind the data become foundations for exploring relevant and effective solutions.

A cursory overview of the table, even without the accompanying detailed reports, offers rich possibilities for community discourse. When faced with a report such as this, the community groups who will review and discuss the data should consider a number of focused questions to guide their deliberations, such as the following:

1. What is the purpose of the data review?

2. Is the group satisfied that the data are accurate, inclusive, reliable, and valid?

3. Item by item, consider these issues:

    A. Examine detailed reports regarding how many children are in the categories of response to this item; how severe is this issue?

    B. What does the data indicate about children's strengths? Vulnerabilities?

    C. What are the standards by which the group assesses the indicator (e.g., comparison to another community or normative group; community opinion; trends over time)? Standards may be relative to an absolute level (e.g., no drug use is acceptable) to relative to other groups (i.e., this seems typical for children this age).

    D. When current data are compared to past data and the trend analysis over time, is the indicator suggesting child well-being is getting better or worse? What are the possible reasons for the status and trend of this indicator?

    E. If the indicator or set of indicators suggest an asset that needs to be enhanced or a problem that needs to be reduced, how can the issue be clearly defined?

4. Taken as a group, which indicators suggest the need for community action? Which is highest priority?

5. Based on this data analysis and interpretation, what courses of community action seem to be appropriate? What is the logic behind the alternative courses?

6. Which course of action is most likely to lead to the group's vision of child well-being in the community?

7. What is the consensus about the most appropriate and feasible course of action?

After communities review their child well-being indicators, the next step is to develop an action plan to promote community resources so that children's well-being can be maintained or enhanced. The plan leads to implementation, evaluation, and re-assessment.

To illustrate part of this process, a hypothetical group discussion about selected data from Table 1 will be described. A Children's Council from Smithville has observed that 10 percent of children ages 10-13 have used illegal drugs more than twice, down from 13 percent 2 years earlier. In the opinion of the group, the trend is positive but the absolute rate is unacceptable. They note that children may be inclined to take risks because only about a third of the children have high life satisfaction and may be drained or bored. They are in academic activities for over 10 hours each day and 97 percent feel they rarely are with peers or can choose what they want to do. Along with their review of other relevant information, the council decides their community has fallen short of meeting its vision of being a place where children are responsible and efficacious. They decide to help children have more balance in their lives: less academic time, more free time with friends or pursuing personal interests. They develop an action plan to pursue the creation of those opportunities.

Meanwhile, the Jonesville Children's Council is pleased that over the last 6 years, their efforts to create more creative and athletic activities of children has led to an increase in children's reports of self confidence about these activities and they have created more "hang out" areas for young people. They are still concerned that the rates are lower than they would like (according to their community vision) so they will continue through their action plan to try to increase these responses. They note that all the rates for risk behaviors are lower than in the past (positive trends), but still unacceptable.

Clearly, the data for Smithville and Jonesville could be mined for weeks and stimulate intense discussion and action. Using two examples illustrates how absolute values for each community cannot be directly compared; the most significant interpretation is in the context of the community, its past, and future projections.

CONCLUSIONS

Measuring and monitoring child well-being at the community level must occur in the context of comprehensive community planning, organizing, and action in pursuit of a vision about the quality of children's lives. The use of our suggested indicators for children's well-being can stimulate ideas about factors to include in the community vision and feasible ways to pursue making the vision become reality. Emphasis should be on the child, although family and communi: · resources should also be monitored.

The pursuit of well-being requires communal will and investment of resources in the form of materials, time, and skills (e.g., assessment, information processing, group facilitation, leadership). A fair and equitable effort must be inclusive, which requires building bridges among diverse sectors of the community. This effort cannot be ad hoc, simply based in a time-limited response to an immediate need or call for action. To be effective, the effort must be sustained over time.

In this information age, there may be temptation to create child well-being indicators in a relative vacuum, independent of potential users or community context. Such an enterprise may produce impressive documents and web pages, but if they exist primarily in cyberspace or in someone's file cabinet, they are barely worth the investment to produce them. Data that becomes a routine part of community dialogue and is "owned" by those most affected by it becomes a vital and viable resource, a tool in the complex mechanisms that lead to lasting and positive change. Designers of systems to measure and monitor child well-being at the community level are advised to place the designs in the broader community-change context.

CHAPTER 8

MEASURING AND MONITORING CHILDREN'S WELL-BEING AND THE MAKING OF POLICY

By now it should be clear: we strongly, believe that any effort to measure and monitor children's well-being is justified by its positive direct and indirect impact on children's lives. Knowing for the sake of knowing, planning, and even monitoring is not enough. Measuring children's well-being should be undertaken for the sake of improving the state of the child.

In the previous chapter, we discussed in depth the use of measuring and monitoring for community-level planning and action. It is now time to move forward to the larger context, that of the policy-making arena. It is evident that some indicators and measurements have led to new policies and programs for children, and some have not (see the section on possible benefits from such an effort in Chapters 1 and 2 for more details). It is also evident that the same indicator when used in some countries and instances has led to desired outcomes, while in other places it did not. So we are left with the question: which are the best indicators of children's well-being? Furthermore, we face another question: are there any rules or guidelines for how an indicator should and could be constructed? How can the knowledge gained from using the indicator be brought into policy-making decisions?

Identifying such indicators and especially such guidelines will enable us to measure the state of the child effectively, which means measuring in order to understand and improve the lives of children. Toward that end, our international project has taken two approaches. First, we have conducted five case studies on the use of indicators of child poverty and family economic well-being to change social policies-- in Ireland, South Africa, France, Israel and the United States. We hoped to learn more on the use of indicators for children's well-being by examining in detail the use of such indicators in a number of different countries.

Second, based on the knowledge gained from the case studies as well as from the project participants' experience and knowledge, we have identified appropriate goals and sub-goals for an effective measuring and monitoring effort. Furthermore, we developed criteria for indicators of children's well-being that will enhance their policy utility. Finally, we attempted to study the

A. Ben-Arieh et al (eds.), Measuring and Monitoring Children's Well-Being, 119–128.
© 2001 *Kluwer Academic Publishers. Printed in the Netherlands.*

conditions that foster or obstruct the use of such indicators for the making of policy.

Thus, this chapter is divided into five sections. First we discuss the desired goals, sub-goals and the process of development of any effort to use indicators for influencing the making of policies. Then we present the criteria for indicators of children's well-being that will enhance the utility of the indicators for policy makers. We then discuss the conditions that accompany any such effort and conclude with a short summary.

GOALS, SUB-GOALS, AND THE PROCESS OF DEVELOPMENT

Belief in the value of children's well-being indicators as a mean for improving children's lives should remain at a declarative level. If we want the indicators to be used in policy making, we should take the proper steps in advance. Our experience and knowledge leads us to conclude that in order to succeed, we have to set forward specific goals and sub-goals, as well as to follow a specific pattern of development.

We suggest that any such effort would pursue the following overall goal:
Influence in positive way public and private actions on behalf of children's well-being

Furthermore we suggest the following sub-goals:
Alert society to the current status of children and to past and emerging Trends
Identify sub-groups in which children's well-being has specific characters
Direct to causal factors of changes in children's well-being as policy relevant intervention points
Evaluate policy interventions in terms of their effect on children's well-being
Consider the broader consequences of children's well-being

It is our belief that when such goals are established at the beginning of an effort to measure and monitor the well-being of children, they increase the chances of using those indicators for making positive change. It is also clear from the case studies we examined that such goals are crucial for influencing policies. The positive experience of UNICEF and the World Summit for Children, which began with clearly stated goals, provide evidence of the need for these crucial steps (Grant & Adamson, 1979-1995).

But, stating clear policy-oriented goals is not enough. Our case studies led us to observe the need for two further steps:

Planing must be based on and rooted in the experience of children from all population groups

To develop accurate indicators that yield persuasive results, one must make sure the indicators are relevant. We found that the best way to assure relevancy is to base the development of the indicators on the experience of children. We draw this conclusion from our case studies, particularly from the analysis of poverty indicators, which established the relevance of the experiences of the poor for developing effective child poverty indicators (Habib, 1997; Tardieu, Lopez, & Tardieu, 1998). Furthermore, in order to be relevant to all children, the indicators- development process must be rooted in the experience of all children. We especially emphasize the importance of basing the development process on the experience of poor children and children from other disadvantaged groups (Andrews & Ben-Arieh, 1999).

Planning must be based on and rooted in the public policies debate

Beyond ensuring the relevance of the indicators for children's well-being, it is essential to establish their relevance to the making of policies. In order to do so, the indicators-development process must be rooted in the existing public debate. The indicators would more successfully become a part of the public debate if studies will embark from existing public debates and then feed back into the public debates their results.

CRITERIA FOR INDICATORS

Any list of indicators will have to be tested and approved before used to monitor and measure children's well-being. Beyond establishing that they are morally and theoretically sound, indicators also need to be validated. In the case of indicators of children's well-being, disputes continue over basic issues, for example the definition of *well-being* and the critical domains (see Chapter 4). We suggest a two-stage review process. First the indicators would be checked to determine validity and relevance. Second, indicators would be reviewed for their potential to influence policy making.

Validity and Relevance Criteria for Indicators of Children's Well-being

A number of sets of guidelines or criteria for reviewing indicators of children's well-being have been suggested (Moore, 1997; Raphael, Renwick, Brown, & Rootman, 1996). They all share the goal of suggesting ways to develop better indicators to measure and monitor children's well-being. Based on earlier work, our case studies, and the mutual experience and knowledge of our international group, we developed the following criteria. We have not tried to rank them in order of importance since they all are relevant and need to be considered:

Significance for the well-being of children
Indicators of children's well-being should not only be valid. They also need to be comprehensive in their coverage of well-being issues, and they must be related to significant consequences for the children's well-being. It would be a serious mistake to focus on insignificant aspects of children's lives and well-being.

Conceptually valid
Any indicator for children's well-being should be based on solid conceptual grounds. This is especially important due to the lack of consensus on the meaning of well-being and the lack of agreement on a single theoretical framework.

Accurate
It is crucial to have accurate indicators. Given the disputes about definitions and domains of children's well-being, we must carefully avoid any lack of accuracy that might diminish our efforts. Furthermore, the indicators should accurately reflect the importance of the status of children's well-being and not accept a vague and over simplified estimations as a compromise.

Clearly interpretable and understandable
We cannot expect professionals, policy makers, and the general public to spend time trying to understand complex statistical measures of children's well-being. If we want the indicators to gain credibility, they must be clearly, easily, and readily understood.

Provides basis for appreciating the consequences
A valid and good indicator would not only measure the current status of children's well-being. Monitoring the trends is important. Building a base for monitoring future trends and thus analyzing consequences of existing policies or programs is crucial.

Relate to sources and outcomes
A good indicator would relate both to the sources of the current status of children and to the likely outcomes for children of existing policies and programs.

Robust to criticism
For any indicator to be taken seriously, it would have to be perceived by critics in the research community and by decision makers across the political spectrum as fair, accurate, and unbiased. If not, debate is likely to focus on the indicator rather than the conclusions of the study and what should be done.

We believe that if such criteria are used to evaluate children's well-being, indicators the result will be positive. Such indicators, based on such criteria, will be valid and useful for dramatically improving our knowledge about children's lives and well-being.

Nevertheless, the focus of this chapter is on the contribution of those indicators to the making of policies. As mentioned before, we further propose an additional set of criteria that will enhance the policy utility of the indicators. One list of criteria should not be used without the other, thus the policies-oriented list would be a waste of time if the basic criteria are not applied as well. Similarly, if the basic criteria are used alone, the effort will result in a valid list of indicators which would have little utility in affecting the making of policy.

Policy Utility Criteria for Indicators of Children's Well-being

Relevant to policy variables
We propose that the basic criteria for making an indicator policy oriented would be its relevance to recognized policy variables.

Compelling to media and to advocacy groups
If we want our indicators to be used to influence policies, they must be understandable by and compelling to the media and to advocacy groups. This will ensure that the data collected will enter into the public debate.

Persuasive to policy makers
Furthermore, policy-oriented indicators should be compelling to policy makers on all levels and across social and political institutions.

Collectible and assessable by operational units
If the indicators are to be used, then the data cannot be collected in remote and isolated places. It must be collected by and be available to responsible agencies in the public and private sectors and at all levels. If we want those who are working with children to use the indicators for their work and planning, they must be able to collect and access the data by themselves.

Challenge stereotypes that were obstacles to action
We know that stereotypes are an obstacle to changing policies. For example assumptions that the poor are lazy and neglect their children, can prevent action for improving poor children's well-being. If we want to change policies, our indicators must challenge uninformed beliefs and stereotypes that are known to be obstacles to action.

Finally we suggest a three-fold validity check.

Validity check for children's well-being indicators

Face Validity
Indicators must be clearly understandable to and interpretable by the educated lay public (at a minimum) and the general public (ideally).

Predictive validity
Indicators should be constructed in a way that changes in the indicators measurements could be used to discuss changes in the well-being of children, youth, and society in the future.

Post-dictive validity
Similarly, indicators should be constructed so that changes in social, economic, and/or policies factors would predict change in the measured indicator.

Thus, it is our belief that when such criteria are used to review any given list of indicators of children's well-being the result will not only be better and more robust indicators, but also that such indicators will have a greater potential of making a difference in children lives. Furthermore, it is evident that various associated conditions contribute to or harm the prospects of using indicators of children's well-being for the making of policies. The next section explores this issue.

ASSOCIATED FACILITATING CONDITIONS

It is evident from our own five case studies that there are a number of associated conditions and forces that interact with the indicators and their usage (Aber, 1997; Frazer, 1998; Habib, 1997; Tardieu et al., 1998). It is therefore our intention in the following section to describe such conditions and suggest how they can be used to facilitate improvements in children's well-being.

Agents of change as mediators
We found that when agents of change, such as advocacy groups, opinion leaders, or high-ranking bureaucrats, are involved in the process of measuring and monitoring children's well-being, they tend to act as mediators between the producers of the data and decision makers. When acting as mediators, they are making a commitment not only for the cause but also for making good use of the power of information.

Accompany the indicator by analysis and data relevant to appropriate responses
When releasing data, one should be ready to take advantage of the opportunity of capturing the public attention to put forward appropriate responses to the current situation as reflected by the use of the indicator. Too many times, those who use the indicator may make a strong case using their data but are not successful at explaining and arguing for appropriate policy changes. Making use of the release of data to also recommend policy

reforms will enhance the likelihood that policy makers will include the data in the policy-making process.

Accompany the indicator with efforts to address criticisms and doubts about its validity
In a similar way, when an indicator is used to measure and monitor children's well-being, a natural and expected response would be criticism of the indicator. If we want to have an impact, we must be ready to defend the indicator's validity.

Consensus about how to respond
Too many times, we establish widespread agreement on the status of children's well-being, but disagree on the appropriate strategies for improving that status. If a consensus is formed on how to proceed in the making of policies, the likelihood that the data will have an impact will be enhanced.

Integrated strategic communications campaign
Influencing the making of policies requires sophisticated strategies. Just as we cannot be careless in our efforts to construct the best indicators for children's well-being, we cannot be careless in our efforts to make the most of the indicators. We must plan an integrated strategic campaign making use in a sophisticated and sustained way of the knowledge of child advocacy groups about how to make best use of media connections.

Preparedness for long-term sustained efforts (at least 5 to 10 years)
Finding good and accurate indicators for children's well-being is a long and tedious process. Influencing policies and making a difference in children's well-being is likely to be an even longer and certainly more frustrating process. If we want to make a difference, we must be prepared for a long-term effort. If such an effort can not be sustained for at least a number of years, then we might reconsider making an effort at all.

Interested political forces
Even when all the criteria and conditions appear favorable for making a desired change in children's lives, such a change is not assured. The political arena, where the policy-making process takes place, is complicated by

various interests and players. Building an alliance of concerned political groups is an important step for the effective use of children's well-being indicators.

Favorable economic conditions and ideological atmosphere

Policy making is always contingent on the existing economic conditions. We know that when resources are scarce the chances of influencing policies are lower, even with very persuasive indicators and data. On the contrary, when resources are abundant, the same data can be very useful for changing policies. Similarly, ideological conditions can foster or impede the use of good indicators and data to influence policies.

Finally, there are three additional questions about the impact of children's well-being indicators on policies.

How important are international comparisons?

Data on this issue are mixed. We know that in a number of important areas international comparisons were found to be extremely useful in bringing about change (Bottani, 1994; Gottschalk, Smeeding, 1995; Smeeding & Gottschalk, 1995). In other cases, international comparison appears not to make a difference. It seems that especially in the United States, international comparisons have not proved significant (Aber, 1996).

How much information is needed?

In some cases, too much information may desensitize the public. Even in an information era, too much information can be harmful. The paradox is that we are in a period when the public is educated and able to accumulate large amounts of sophisticated information. But because the information is presented in a fragmented and dramatized way (usually by the media), good, reliable, and useful information is short in supply.

Are indicators universal and timeless or time- and place-specific?

Once again this is probably a question of avoiding the extremes. We have argued for indicators that can be used consistently and would enable the monitoring of trends. We have also argued for indicators rooted in the policy arena and within the particular political context. This issue is related to the perspective, duration, and the desired impact of the indicator, and the answer lies in the specific indicator, the context, and the expected use.

CHAPTER 8

CONCLUSIONS

There should be no doubt that an effort to measure and monitor children's well-being can have an impact on the making of policies. In fact, we know from our case studies and those of others that measuring and monitoring can be effective (see Chapters 1 and 2 for more details). However, the nature and degree of the impact would be contingent on many intervening factors. Many of those intervening factors could be addressed and dealt with by whoever is collecting the data and is interested in promoting the well-being of children.

In this chapter, we have dealt with issues that might affect how and whether one's findings are used or ignored in the policy-making process. We acknowledge that some of these factors are beyond the control of those who collect the data and work with it to improve children's well-being. However, it is crucial that these factors be recognized and their consequences carefully considered.

CHAPTER 9

SUMMARY AND AGENDA FOR THE FUTURE

In the previous eight chapters, we have tried to convey a message, a message that measuring and monitoring children's well-being is a feasible task. Furthermore, it is a vital task for anyone who wishes to positively affect children's well-being.

In this chapter, we would like to reflect on our message. We have divided the chapter into four sections. After this brief preamble we turn to deal with the question of what this is all about. Discussing the international project that led to the publication of this book follows, and finally we suggest an agenda for the future.

WHAT WAS THIS ALL ABOUT?

A simple glance at the title of this book leads to the answer that it was all about measuring and monitoring children's well-being-- yet there is more. This book is about knowledge and information. It is about the power of information and its use; it is about learning from others and learning from children; and it is about well-being and its measurement. But most of all, it is about children and how we can positively affect their lives in their communities and at large.

We have started by laying before the reader the rationale for measuring and monitoring children's well-being. From the beginning we have argued in favor of measuring for the sake of doing. The emphasis on measuring and monitoring as tools for affecting children's well-being is incorporated throughout the book.

We then turned to the work of others in this field. We have presented the most extensive picture we could assemble from around the world, to indicate that we have learned and will continue to learn from others, and to show that the necessary work has begun and our objectives can be achieved.

A. Ben-Arieh et al (eds.), Measuring and Monitoring Children's Well-Being, 129–134.
© 2001 *Kluwer Academic Publishers. Printed in the Netherlands.*

We would like to think of the book as a journey, a journey that did not take us down the easily travelled paved paths, but rather to new paths that will lead to improvements in children's lives.

We shared our basic principles and guidelines with you, the reader, not with claims that they are the only useful ones, but rather as suggestions for your consideration. We accompanied them with a solid rationale and our research foundation. We have recommended the concept of children's well-being as a new challenge for academic researchers, professionals, and policy makers. We have developed and explained our selection of five domains for measuring and monitoring children's well-being and the indicators we suggest to use in each. All of them are well grounded in theory and values. We cherish the value support as much as the research.

We also suggested practical ways to carry out the tasks involved, and the need to collect data from various sources about the different characteristics and purposes of these sources. We have tried to be ambitious, but also practical; therefore, we presented our ideas and rationale as well as examples of where the task is already being undertaken.

We combined the practical tasks with our new strategies and concepts, and laid out fifty indicators for children's well-being along with their rationale, research support, and measurement.

But, most of all our work is about children. Our focus has led us to suggest how measuring and monitoring efforts can be used to promote children's well-being through their communities and how policies could be positively affected.

If we had to distill our work to a one-line description, it would undoubtedly be – how can we learn more about children's lives and how do we focus attention on children in order to bring about positive change in their everyday lives?

THE INTERNATIONAL PROJECT

We have referred numerous times to one international project. We were referring to the international project "Monitoring and Measuring Children's Well-Being" (see Chapter 2 for a full description). We have done so not only because this book is one of the project outcomes.

We have referred to this project because we truly believe it has changed our way of thinking, paved new roads, and introduced new concepts into the field. This project was a truly extraordinary experience for us, one that had great influence on our work. We hope that the ideas and concepts we found to be so appealing and promising will evoke a similar response in our readers.

THE FUTURE

Making progress on new roads must not distract us from continuously looking at how to better pave them or even locating better roads. In that regard, we see special merit in explicating our prospects for the future. We would like to do so while looking at four different issues: prospects for future research, an agenda for future actions, prospects for stronger communities, and--last, but certainly not least--improving the lives of children.

Future Research

We would be the first to acknowledge that much work is still to be done in order to fully utilize what is presented here. In many ways, the vindication of all our work lies ahead. We see the need for future research in two main aspects: elaborating and specifying the concept of children's well-being, and carrying out the measurement through actual collection and analysis of data.

The concepts

We believe the concepts and basic assumptions that were presented here are theoretically sound (see Chapters 3 and 4), but they should also be seen as pointing us in the right direction for future work. The concepts of children's rights, childhood as a stage of itself, the child as a unit of observation and the other concepts described in depth in Chapters 3 and 4 are likely to be challenged by very strong and traditional concepts of children's well-being and childhood. The dispute is far from being resolved, and thus we foresee that much more work will be needed to establish these concepts and to gain wider support for them.

This future research must be both theoretical and empirical. There is an obvious need to continue to develop and define the basic concepts of childhood as a stage in and of itself as well as of children's rights. Furthermore, although moral support is important, empirical findings that will support these concepts will be of great value and thus should be a major focus of future research.

The measurements

It is evident that much work lies ahead in order to transform the list of indicators presented in this book into a practical set of measurement devices. Furthermore, we cannot accomplish this goal until we actually go into the field and test our selected indicators and measurements. It is our plan, therefore, that the international project will evolve into a multinational cluster of studies, focusing on children's well-being in the context of an international comparative framework.

The collection of data

From our work, it is evident that although we know a great deal about children's lives we do not know enough. It should also be stated clearly that much of the data we need can only be collected through new studies and surveys. We, therefore, have placed on our agenda for the future the conduct of a periodical (every 3-7 years) study of children and childhood. Such a study would have to be based on the concepts elaborated in Chapters 3 and 4 and would have to use the child as a unit of observation.

Furthermore, we call for studies that would enlighten us about children's daily activities and especially their time use. We foresee the need for conducting special public opinion polls among children, similar to studies already conducted among adults, and we believe there is a need to look carefully at subjective dimensions of children's well-being in addition to objective information being gathered. To sum up, we can say that the future agenda for collecting data on children's well-being is one in which we focus on the children, asking them directly and respecting them as equal human beings.

Agenda for Future Actions

It is our hope that future actions to promote children's well-being will be based on research that will supply better knowledge about children's lives. But the need for further information should not be an excuse for inaction. It is evident from the data we have today that children's well-being is in danger--not only among the majority of the world where children live in developing countries, but also among children living in the most rich and industrialized countries.

We therefore call for a close collaboration between data collectors and policy makers. There is an obvious need to use the power of information to improve children's well-being. We further call for a closer collaboration between data collectors and child advocates. We must find and develop the best ways to use our knowledge to mobilize those who are working to improve children's well-being. In this endeavor, child advocates are our natural partners and very capable ones. Finally, we call for a closer collaboration with professionals and better dissemination of data and our analysis of it to professionals and whoever else works with children.

Prospects for Community Work

It is evident that much of the effort towards measuring and monitoring children's well-being is being done at the international, national, or regional level. It is also evident that children's communities influence their well-being. Thus, we must find ways to collaborate with communities and community workers. Moreover, we must base our data collection on communities' values and analyze the data in community context and then provide feedback about the data to the communities to help them plan action in the community.

Communities are powerful partners in defining children's well-being and in collecting the data we need, but more important is the ability of the community to positively affect the well-being of children.

THE CHILDREN

There could be no better topic with which to conclude this book than that of the children themselves. Our agenda for the future of children is simple and clear. First we must acknowledge that our work is all about children and their well-being. Children's well-being is the ultimate goal of any effort to measure and monitor children's status.

Then we must be honest with ourselves. Speaking about children's rights, focusing on the child and childhood as a stage of itself will serve no purpose if we do not employ these concepts and principles in our own work.

A future agenda will therefore, be an agenda where children are full partners in all stages of the effort. Children should be involved from the very beginning of any effort to measure and monitor their well-being. They should be a part of identifying the values and the indicators. They should be a part of collecting the data; they should be a part of analyzing the data and its implications; and they should be a part of the action to positively change their lives.

APPENDIX 1: STATE OF THE CHILD REPORTS FROM AROUND THE WORLD

We acknowledge the fact that additional reports exist, and that due to our linguistic skills we might have missed a number of reports especially in the Latin languages

Adair, Peggy. *Hide & seek : the state of the child in Nebraska*. Omaha, NE: Voices for Children in Nebraska, 1992.

Adamson, Peter, and Petra Morrison, eds. *The Progress of Nations*. New York: UNICEF, 1995.

Ahmed, Kazi A., Brenda Johnson, and Beverly Blegen. *North Dakota's children : a chart book perspective, 1993*. Bismarck, N.D.: Children and Family Services Division North Dakota Dept. of Human Services, 1993.

Alaska Committee on Children and Youth. *Children and youth in Alaska, the 49th State; official report*. Juneau, Alaska: The Committee, 1959.

Alaska Division of Family and Youth Services. *Children in crisis : a report on runaway and homeless youth in Alaska*. Juneau, Alaska: The Division, 1992.

Barnhorst, Richard, and Laura C. Johnson, eds. *The State of the Child in Ontario*. Toronto: The Child Youth and Family Policy Research Center , Oxford University Press, 1991.

Bellamy, Carol. *The state of the world's children*. New York: Oxford University Press, 1996-1999.

Ben-Arieh, Asher, ed. *The State of the Child in Israel - A Statistical Abstract*. Jerusalem: National Council for the Child, 1992-1995.

Ben-Arieh, Asher, and Yaffa Zionit, eds. *The State of the Child in Israel*. Jerusalem: National Council for the Child, 1996-1999.

Canada Dominion Bureau of Statistics, Health and Welfare Division. *Selected statistics on children*. Ottawa: Dominion Bureau of Statistics Census and Health and Welfare Divisions, 1965.

Children's Defense Fund. *The state of America's children*. Washington, D.C.: Children's Defense Fund, 1991-1999.

Child Welfare League of America. *Investing in the Future: Promoting the Well-being of North Dakota's Children and Families*. Washington D.C.: CWLA, 1994.

Department of Health and Human Services. *Healthy Children 2000*. Springfield, VA: Department of Health and Human Services, 1999.

Dereje, Asrat. *The state of Africa's children : priorities for action : a report*. Nairobi: UNICEF, 1988.

El Deeb, Bothayna. *The State of Egyptian children, June 1988*. Cairo: UNICEF, 1988.

Fayyazuddin, Samra, Anees Jillani, and Zarina Jillani. *The state of Pakistan's children, 1997*. 1st ed. Islamabad: Sparc, 1998.

Federal Interagency Forum on Child and Family Statistics. *America's children : key national indicators of well-being*. Washington, D.C.: The Forum, 1997.

Florida. Legislature. House of Representatives. Ad Hoc Committee on Children. *1988 the state of Florida's children and families*. Tallahassee, FL.: Florida House of Representatives Ad Hoc Committee on Children, 1988.

Gale Research Inc. *Statistical record of children*. Detroit: Gale Research, 1994.

Goerge, Robert, Fred Wulczyn, and Allen Harden. *A Report from the Multistate Foster Care Data Archive*. Chicago: Chapin Hall Center for Children at the University of Chicago, 1994.

Grant, James P., and Peter Adamson. *The state of the world's children*. New York: Oxford University Press, 1979-1995.

Hawaii. Maternal and Child Health Services Branch. *Health characteristics of children and youth : partial results of a state-federal survey conducted on the Island of Oahu during the year October 1958-September 1959, Hawaii health survey report ; no. 5*. Hawaii: Maternal and Child Health Services Branch, 1962.

Hernandez, Donald J., and Evan Charney. *From generation to generation : the health and well-being of children in immigrant families*. Washington, DC: National Academy Press, 1998.

Hilsum, Lindsey. *State of South Africa's children : an agenda for action*. Johannesburg: National Children's Rights Committee, 1993.

Hobbs, Frank, and Laura Lippman. *Children's well-being : an international comparison, International population reports*. Washington, D.C.: U.S. Dept. of Commerce Bureau of the Census, 1990.

Horner, Mary P., and Kevin Crowe. *Nevada's children : selected educational and social statistics, Nevada and national*. Carson City, Nev.: Nevada Dept. of Education, 1992.

Howell, Frank M., Paul Randall Vowell, J. and Gipson Wells. *Indicators of the well-being of Mississippi children, Social research report series ; 98-1*. Mississippi State: Mississippi State University Social Science Research Center, 1998.

Hughes, Dana. *The Health of America's children : maternal and child health data book*. Washington, D.C.: Children's Defense Fund, 1987.

Indonesia. Menteri Koordinator Bidang Kesejahteraan Rakyat. *State of children in Indonesia*. Jakarta: Kantor Menteri Koordinator Bidang Kesejahteraan Rakyat, 1991.

Janet, M. Simons, Belva Finaly, and Alice Yang. *The Adolescent & Young Adult Fact Book*. Washington D.C.: Children Defense Fund, 1991.

Jensen, An-Magritt, and Angelo Saporiti. *Do Children Count?* Vol. 36/17, *Eurosocial report*. Vienna: European Center for Social Welfare Policy and Research, 1992.

Kampen, Jacob van, M. Beker, and Dies Wilbrink-Griffioen. *The state of the young Netherlands : a national report on the situation of children and young people in the Netherlands, commissioned by the Interdepartmental Commission for Youth Research*. Delft: Eburon Publishers, 1996.

Kameya, Lawrence I. *The state of children's services data in the state of Ohio : a report to the Ohio Commission for Children*. Columbus, OH: Ohio Commission for Children, 1980.

Kids Count (Project). *City kids count : data on the well-being of children in large cities*. Baltimore, MD: Annie E. Casey Foundation, 1997.

Knitzer, Jane, and Stephen Page. *Map and track : state initiatives for young children and families*. 1998 ed. New York: National Center for Children in Poverty, 1996-1998.

Kogan, Leonard S., and Shirley Jenkins. *Indicators of child health and welfare; development of the DIPOV index*. New York,: Center for Social Research Graduate Center City University of New York, 1974.

Kornreich, Toby, Linda Sandler, and Duane Hall. *Kids Count fact book : Arizona's children, 1992*. Tempe, Ariz.: The Morrison Institute for Public Policy, 1992.

Lazarus, Wendy. *California, the state of our children, 1989 : where we stand & where we go from here*. Los Angeles: Children Now, 1989.

Le Bras, Herv. *Child and family : demographic developments in the OECD countries*. Paris: Organisation for Economic Co-operation and Development, 1979.

Maryland 4-C Committee. *Statistics on Maryland's children and their families; a report.* Baltimore, 1973.

Massachusetts Legislative Children's Caucus. *The state of Massachusetts children and youth.* Boston, MA: The Caucus, 1994.

Massachusetts. Dept. of Public Health. *Massachusetts's children & youth : a status report.* Boston, MA: The Dept., 1995.

Miringhoff, Marc L., and Sandra Opdycke. *The Index of Social Health: Monitoring the Social Well-being of Children in Industrialized Countries: A Report to UNICEF.* New York: The Fordham Institute for Innovation in Social Policy, 1993.

Morrison Institute for Public Policy. *The state of Arizona's children 1996 : Kids Count.* Phoenix, Ariz.: Children's Action Alliance, 1996.

National Institute of Public Cooperation and Child Development. *Statistics on children in India : pocket book.* 4th rev. ed. New Delhi: National Institute of Public Cooperation and Child Development, 1993.

National Institute of Public Cooperation and Child Development. *Statistics on children in India : pocket book 1990.* 1st ed. New Delhi: National Institute of Public Cooperation and Child Development, 1990.

National Institute of Public Cooperation and Child Development. *Statistics on children in India pocket book.* 5th rev. ed. New Delhi: National Institute of Public Cooperation and Child Development, 1994.

New Caledonia South Pacific Commission. *State of Pacific children.* Noumea, New Caledonia South Pacific Commission, 1993., 1993.

New York State Council on Children and Families. *State of the child in New York State.* Albany, N.Y.: The Council, 1988.

North Carolina Child Advocacy Institute. *Children's Index 1993: A Profile of Leading Indicators of the Health and Well-being of North Carolina's Children.* North Carolina: North Carolina Child Advocacy Institute, 1993.

North Carolina. Office of Child Development., and George Penick. *The state of young children in North Carolina : a compilation of needs and services, 1974.* [Raleigh]: North Carolina Office of Child Development Dept. of Administration, 1974.

Norwegian Commissioner for Children. *Facts about Children in Norway.* Oslo: Norwegian Commissioner for Children, 1990.

Real, Mark. *Creating Futures for Ohio's Children.* Columbus: Junior Leagues of Ohio, 1991.

Regina Council on Social Development. *The state of Regina's children : report from the community.* Regina: The Council, 1993.

Rosenbaum, Sara. *The Health of America's children, 1991 : state and city data appendix to CDF's Child, Youth and Family Futures Clearinghouse report.* Washington, D.C.: Children's Defense Fund, 1991.

Rosenbaum, Sara, Christine Layton, and Joseph Liu. *The Health of America's Children.* Washington D.C.: Children Defense Fund, 1991.

Schmittroth, Linda. *Statistical record of children.* Detroit: Gale Research, 1994.

Shamgar-Handelman, Lea. *Childhood as a Social Phenomenon: National Report Israel.* Vol. 36/15, *Childhood as a Social Phenomenon.* Vienna: European Center for Social Welfare Policy and Research, 1990.

Simkin, Linda. *Child and adolescent health profile, New York State, 1987.* Albany, NY (Empire State Plaza, Albany 12237): Copies from Bureau of Child and Adolescent Health, 1989.

138

South Carolina. State Budget and Control Board. Office of Research and Statistics. *Kids count South Carolina : 1996 report*. [Columbia: State Budget and Control Board Office of Research and Statistics, 1996.

Tennessee Kids Count (Organisation), and Tennessee. Commission on Children and Youth. *The county report : [a county-by-county report on the well-being of Tennessee's children]*. Nashville, Tenn.: Tennessee Commission on Children & Youth Tennessee Kids Count, 1993.

Testa, Mark, and Edward Lawlor. *The State of the Child 1985*. Chicago: Chapin Hall Center for Children at the University of Chicago, 1985.

Testa, Mark, and Fred Wulczyn. *The state of the child, A Series of research reports on children in Illinois ; v. 1*. Chicago, Ill.: Children's Policy Research Project School of Social Service Administration The University of Chicago, 1980.

UNICEF Angola. *The state of Angola's children report*. Luanda: UNICEF Angola, 1995.

United States. Congress. D.C. Financial Responsibility and Management Assistance Authority. *Children in crisis : statistics, facts, and figures*. Washington, D.C.: The Authority, 1996.

United States. Congress. House. Select Committee on Children Youth and Families. *Children's well-being : an international comparison : a report of the Select Committee on Children, Youth, and Families, One Hundred First Congress, second session, together with additional minority views*. Washington D.C.: G.P.O., 1990.

United States. Indian Health Service., *Final report, profile of the state of Indian children and youth : in support of the Domestic Policy Council Workgroup on Indian Youth, for and on the behalf of Indian Health Service, Department of Health and Human Service*. Silver Spring, MD: Support Services International, 1997.

United States. Indian Health Service. *Final Report, Profile Of The State Of Indian Children And Youth, Etc., November 1997*. Washington D.C.: Indian Health Service, 1998.

Virginia. State Crime Commission. *Children and youth in trouble in Virginia : phase II, a report*. Richmond, VA.: The Commission, 1979.

Virginia. State Crime Commission., and Children and Youth in Trouble in Virginia Advisory Group. *Children and youth in trouble in Virginia : a report*. Richmond, VA.: The Commission, 1977.

Zionit, Yaffa, and Asher Ben-Arieh. *The State of the New Immigrant Children in Israel*. Jerusalem: National Council for the Child, 1995.

APPENDIX 2: THE INTERNATIONAL PROJECT - LIST OF MEMBERS

Aber Larry - National Center for Children in Poverty, Columbia University School of Public Health, USA

Adamson Peter - UNICEF, P&LA,

Andrews (Bowers) Arlene – Institute for Families in Society, University of South Carolina

Armstrong Mary L - Division of State and Local Support, Louis de la Parte Florida Mental Health Institute, University of South Florida, USA

Barell Vita – Health Services Reseatch Unit, Ministry of Health, Chaim Sheba Medical Center, Israel

Ben-Arieh Asher – Center for Research & Public Education, National Council for the Child, Israel

Bistrup Marie Louise - Research coordinator, Childwatch International

Brown Brett - Senior Research Associate, Child Trends, Inc., USA

Callaghan Lucienne - Kopanang Consortium Project - Partnerships in Learning, South Africa

Casas Ferran - Research Institute on Quality of Life Universitat de Girona, Spain

Dolev Talal - Center for Children and Youth, JDC-Brookdale Institute, Israel

Frazer Hugh - Ireland's Combat Poverty Agency

Freguia Cristina – Istat, Italy

Friedman L. Herbert - International Youth Foundation

Froenes Ivar - Instituttet for Sociologi, Universitetet I Oslo, Norway

Furstenberg Frank F. Jr. - Department of Sociology, University of Pennsylvania, USA

Gajst Idith - Centeral Bureau of Statistics, Israel

Giovanni B. Sgritta - Dipertimento di Scienze Demografiche, Universita di Roma "La Sapienza", Italy

Goerge Robert - Chapin Hall Center for Children at the Chicago University, USA

Golinowska Stanislawa - Institute of Labour and Social Studies, Poland

Habib Jack - JDC-Brookdale Institute, Israel

Hassall Ian – (Former) Commissioner for children, New Zealand

Hauge Ingvild - Department for Population & Education Statistics, Statistisk Sentralbyra (Bureau of Statistics), Norway

Hernandez Donald J. - Housing and Household Economic Statistics Division, U.S. Bureau of Census,

Honwana Alicinda Department of Social Anthropology, University of Cape Town, South Africa

Irby Merita - International Youth Foundation

Jensen An-Magritt - Department of Sociology and Political Science (ISS), Norges teknisk-naturvitenskapelige universitet (NTNU), Norway

Lee Bong Joo - Chapin Hall at the University of Chicago, USA

Kadman Yitzhak - National Council for the Child, Israel

Katz Chana – JDC- Israel

Kaufman Natalie (Lee Jane) - Institute for Family and Neighborhood Life, Clemson University, USA

Kidder Karen - The Canadian Institute of Child Health

Kilmartin Christine - Australian Institute of Family Studies

Korvarik Jiri - Research Institute of Labour and Social Affairs, Czech Republic

Lippman Laura - National Center for Education Statistics, USA

Luttrell Carol Ann - Massachusetts Tax Revenue, USA

McDonald Peter - Australian National University

Melton Gary - Institute for Family and Neighborhood Life, Clemson University, USA

Miljeteig Per - Childwatch International

Nauck Bernhard - Department of Sociology, Chemnitz University of Technology, Germany

Pittman Karen - International Youth Foundation

Prout Alan - The Centre for the Social Study of Childhood, School of Comparative and Applied Social Sciences, University of Hull, UK

Qvortrup Jens - Department of Social and Health Studies, South Jutland University Center, Denmark

Rosenfeld Jona M. - JDC-Brookdale Institute, Center for Children and Youth, Israel

Salole Gerry - Programme Doucumentation and Communication, Bernard van Leer Foundation

Saporiti Angelo - Associate Professor of Sociology, University of Molise Universit' degli Studi del Molise, Facult' di Economia (Faculty of Economics), Italy

Sauli Hannele - Bureau of Statistics, Finland

September Roseline - Institute for Child and Family Development, University of Western Cape, South Africa

Smeeding Tim - Center for Policy Research, Maxwell School, Syracuse University, USA

Tardieu Bruno - International Movement ATD - Fourth World

Tipper Jenni - Canadian Institute of Child Health

Torney-Purta Judith - Department of Human Development, Universuty of Maryland, USA

Whitten Peter – Eurostat, Luxemburg

Wilson Kathy – Institute for Family and Neighborhood Life, Clemson University, USA

Wintersberger Helmut – European Center, Vienna, Austria

Wu David Y.H. - Department of Anthropology, Chinese University of Hong Kong

Yanez Jesus Leonardo – The Bernhard van Leer Foundation

REFERENCES

Aber, Lawrence J. "Measuring Child Poverty for Use in Comparative Policy Analysis." In *Monitoring and Measuring the State of Children - Beyond Survival*, edited by Asher Ben-Arieh and Helmut Wintersberger, 193-208. Vienna: European Centre for Social Welfare Policy and Research, 1997a.

Aber, Lawrence J. "Using Indicators of Poverty and Economic Distress to Influence Public Policy: A Current Case Study of the U.S.A." Paper presented at the Monitoring and Measuring Children Well Being - Second International Workshop, Campobasso, Italy 1997b.

Aber, Lawrence J., and Stephanie Jones. "Indicators of Positive Development in Early Childhood: Improving Concepts and Measures." In *Indicators of children's well-being*, edited by Robert M. Hauser, Brett V. Brown, and William R. Prosser, 395-408. New York: Russell Sage Foundation, 1997.

Adamson, Peter, and Petra Morrison, eds. *The Progress of Nations*. New York: UNICEF, 1993-1996.

Adler, Patricia A., and Peter Adler. *Peer power: preadolescent culture and identity*. New Brunswick, N.J.: Rutgers University Press, 1998.

Andress, I., and E.C. Roehlkepartain. "Now what do we do?" In *Source Newsletter*. Minneapolis, MN: The Search Institute. 1993.

Andrews, Arlene Bowers. "Assessing Neighbourhood and Community Factors that Influence Children's Well Being." In *Monitoring and Measuring the State of Children - Beyond Survival*, edited by Asher Ben-Arieh and Helmut Wintersberger, 127-142. Vienna: European Centre for Social Welfare Policy and Research, 1997.

Andrews, Arlene Bowers, and Asher Ben-Arieh. "Measuring and Monitoring Children's Well-Being across the World." *Social Work* 44, no. 2 (1999): 105-115.

Andrews, Arlene Bowers, and Natalie Hevener Kaufman, eds. *Implementing the U.N. Convention on the Rights of the Child: A standard of Living Adequate for Development*. Westport, Connecticut: Prager, 1999.

Annie E. Casey Foundation. *Kids Count Data Book: 1999*. Baltimore, MD: Annie E. Casey Foundation, 1999.

Atkinson, A. B., Lee Rainwater, and Timothy M. Smeeding. *Income distribution in advanced economies: evidence from the Luxembourg Income Study*. Syracuse, N.Y.: Maxwell School of Citizenship and Public Affairs Syracuse University, 1995.

Avard, Denise and Jenni Tipper. "Living a Healthy Life: A Holistic Approach to Child Health." In *Monitoring and Measuring the State of Children - Beyond Survival*, edited by Asher Ben-Arieh and Helmut Wintersberger, 255-264. Vienna: European Centre for Social Welfare Policy and Research, 1997.

Banister, Judith. "FDCH Congressional Testimony." Washington DC: US Congress, 1994.

Banting, K.G. *Poverty, politics and policy*. London: Macmillan, 1979.

Barnhorst, Richard, and Laura C. Johnson, eds. *The State of the Child in Ontario*. Toronto: The Child Youth and Family Policy Research Center, Oxford University Press, 1991.

Bauer, R.A. ed. *Social Indicators*. Cambridge, MA: MIT Press, 1966.

Bellamy, Carol. *The state of the world's children*. New York: Oxford University Press, 1996-1999.

144

Ben-Arieh, Asher, ed. *The State of the Child in Israel - A Statistical Abstract*. Jerusalem: National Council for the Child, 1992-1995.

Ben-Arieh, Asher. "Why Bother? The rationale for Measuring the State of Children." In *Monitoring and Measuring the State of Children - Beyond Survival*, edited by Asher Ben-Arieh and Helmut Wintersberger, 29-38. Vienna: European Centre for Social Welfare Policy and Research, 1997.

Ben-Arieh, Asher, and Helmut Wintersberger, eds. *Monitoring and Measuring the State of Children - Beyond Survival*. Vol. 62. Vienna: European Centre for Social Welfare Policy and Research, 1997.

Ben-Arieh, Asher, and Yaffa Zionit, eds. *The State of the Child in Israel - A Statistical Abstract*. Jerusalem: National Council for the Child, 1996-1999.

Ben-Arieh, A. & Ofir, A. *It is time for (more) time-use studies: Studying the daily activities of children* A paper prepared for the Collaborative Center on Children Well Being, 2000

Ben-Arieh, A "Beyond Welfare: Measuring and Monitoring the State of Children – New Trends and Domains" *Social Indicators Research* (forthcoming)

Bennett, Neil G., and Jane Mosley. "Developing Indices of Child Well-Being for the United States." Paper presented at the Conference on Child Well being in Rich and Transition Countries, Luxembourg 1999.

Berger, S. "Introduction." In *The utilization of the social sciences in policy making in the united states*, edited by S. Berger. Paris: OECD, 1980.

Berkowitz, B. "Analyzing community problems." In *Community Tool Box,* edited by Work Group on Health Promotion and Community Development, Chap. 2, Sec. 3. Lawrence, KS: University of Kansas, 1999.

Biderman, A.D. "Social indicators and goals." In *Social Indicators*, edited by R.A. Bauer, 68-153. Cambridge, MA: MIT Press, 1966.

Blake, Judith. *Family Size and Achievement*. Berkeley: University of California Press, 1989.

Bottani, N. "The OECD International Education Indicators." *Assessment in Education* 1, no. 3 (1994) 1-18.

Bradshaw, Jonathan, and Helen Barnes. "How do Nations Monitor the Well-Being of their Children." Paper presented at the Conference on Child Well Being in Rich and Transition Countries, Luxembourg 1999.

Brannen, P. " Research and social policy: political, organizational and cultural constraints." In *The use and abuse of social science*, edited by F. Heller, 157-170. London: Sage, 1986.

Bronfenbrenner, Urie. *The ecology of human development: experiments by nature and design*. Cambridge, Mass.: Harvard University Press, 1979.

Bulmer, M. "The policy process and the place in it of social research." In *Social science and social policy*, edited by M. Bulmer, 3-30. London: Allen & Unwin, 1986.

Center for the Study of Social Policy. "Kids count data book 1993." Washington, D.C.: Center for the Study of Social Policy. 1993.

Child Trends. "Inventory of state of the child reports in the USA - A report to the Annie E. Casey Foundation." Washington DC: Child Trends Inc., 1999.

Children's Defence Fund. *The state of America's children*. Washington, D.C.: Children's Defense Fund, 1991-1999.

Citizens' Committee for Children. "Keeping track of New York city's children.". New York: Citizens' Committee for Children, 1993.

Citro, C., and R. Michael. *Measuring Poverty: A New Approach*. Washington D.C: National Academy of Sciences Press, 1995.

Cornia, Giovani A., and Sheldon Danziger, eds. *Child Poverty and Deprivation in the Industrialized Countries 1945-1995*. Oxford: Clarendon Press, 1997.

Council of Europe. "Age at which Children are Legally entitled to a series of acts." In *Childhood Policies*, edited by Council of Europe, 1996.

Currie, Candace. "Health and Well-Being and Their Association with Affluence and Deprivation Among School-aged Children in Europe and North America: the WHO HBSC 1997/98." Paper presented at the Child Well being in Rich and Transition Countries, Luxembourg 1999.

Danziger, S. , S. Danziger, and J. Stern. "The American Paradox: High Income and High Child Poverty." In *Child Poverty and Deprivation in the Industrialized Countries 1945-1995*, edited by Giovani A. Cornia and Sheldon Danziger, 181-209. Oxford: Clarendon Press, 1997.

De Lone, Richard H. *Small futures : children, inequality, and the limits of liberal reform*. 1st ed. New York: Harcourt Brace Jovanovich, 1979.

De Vylder, Stefan. "Macroeconomic Issues and the Rights of the Child." In *Understanding Children's Rights*, edited by Eugeen Verhellen. Ghent, Belgium: Children's Rights Center, University of Ghent, 1998.

Dolev, Talal, and Jack Habib. "A Conceptual Framework for Developing Indicators." In *Monitoring and Measuring the State of Children - Beyond Survival*, edited by Asher Ben-Arieh and Helmut Wintersberger, 65-80. Vienna: European Centre for Social Welfare Policy and Research, 1997.

Doron, A. "Defining Poverty and its Measurements." *Social Security* 32 (1980): 23-35 (Hebrew).

Duncan, Greg J., and Jeanne Brooks-Gunn, eds. *Consequences of growing up poor*. New York: Russell Sage Foundation, 1997.

Ennew, Judith. "Time for Children or Time for Adults." In *Childhood Matters: Social Theory, Practice and Politics*, edited by Jens Qvortrup, Marita Brady, Giovani Sgritta and Helmut Wintersberger. Aldershot: Avebury, 1994.

Flekkoy, Malfrid Grude, and Natalie Hevener Kaufman. *The Participation Rights of the Child: Rights and Responsibilities in Family and Society*. London: Jessica Kingsley Publishers, 1997.

Flekkoy, Malfrid Grude, and Natalie Hevener Kaufman. "The Social Development of the Child." In *Implementing the U.N. Convention on the Rights of the Child: A standard of Living Adequate for Development*, edited by Arlene Bowers Andrews and Natalie Hevener Kaufman, 117-132. Westport, Connecticut: Prager, 1999.

Frazer, Hugh. "The Use of Social Indicators to Influence Policy in Ireland." Paper presented at the Monitoring and Measuring Children Well Being - The Third International Workshop, Kiawah resort, S.C. USA 1998.

Frones, Ivar. "Children in Modern Families: A Scandinavian Perspective." In *Monitoring and Measuring the State of Children - Beyond Survival*, edited by Asher Ben-Arieh and Helmut Wintersberger, 115-126. Vienna: European Centre for Social Welfare Policy and Research, 1997.

Furstenberg, Frank F. "Family - State Relations and the Well being of Children." In *Monitoring and Measuring the State of Children - Beyond Survival*, edited by Asher Ben-Arieh and Helmut Wintersberger, 187-192. Vienna: European Centre for Social Welfare Policy and Research, 1997.

Furstenberg, Frank F., and Mary E. Huges. "The Influence of Neighborhoods on Children's Development: A Theoretical Perspective and a Research Agenda." In *Indicators of children's well-being*, edited by Robert M. Hauser, Brett V. Brown, and William R. Prosser, 346-377. New York: Russell Sage Foundation , 1997.

Garbarino, James. *Lost boys : why our sons turn violent and how we can save them.* New York: Free Press, 1999.

Garbarino, James. *Raising children in a socially toxic environment.* San Francisco: Jossey-Bass, 1995.

Gershuny, J. "Time Budget Research in Europe." *Statistics in Transition* 2, no. 4 (1995): 517-527.

Goerge, Robert M. "Potential and Problems In Developing Indicators On Child Well Being From Administrative Data." In *Indicators of children's well-being,* edited by Robert M. Hauser, Brett V. Brown, and William R. Prosser, 457-471. New York: Russell Sage Foundation , 1997a.

Goerge, Robert M. "The Use of Administrative Data in Measuring the State of Children." In *Monitoring and Measuring the State of Children - Beyond Survival,* edited by Asher Ben-Arieh and Helmut Wintersberger, 277-286. Vienna: European Centre for Social Welfare Policy and Research, 1997b.

Goerge, Robert M., and Bong Jo Lee, eds. *The state of the child in Illinois.* Chicago: Chapin hall Center for Children, 2000.

Goerge, Robert M., Bong Jo-Lee, T.E. Sommer, and J. Van Voorhis. "The point in time multiple service use of children and adolescents in Illinois." . Chicago: Chapin Hall Center for Children, 1993.

Goerge, Robert M., Fred H. Wulczyn, and Allen W. Harden. "A Report from the Multistate Foster Care Data Archive: Foster care dynamics, 1983-1992." . Chicago: Chapin Hall Center for Children, 1994.

Gottschalk, Peter, and Timothy M. Smeeding. *Cross-national comparisons of levels and trends in inequality.* Syracuse, N.Y.: Maxwell School of Citizenship and Public Affairs Syracuse University, 1995.

Grant, James P., and Peter Adamson. *The state of the world's children.* New York: Oxford University Press, 1979-1995.

Gross, B.M. "Preface." In *Social indicators,* edited by R.A. Bauer, ix-xviii. Cambridge, MA: MIT Press, 1966.

Habib, Jack. "Children in Israel - Social, Educational and economic Perspectives (Hebrew)." . Jerusalem: Henrietta Szold Institute, 1974.

Habib, Jack. "The Experience with Indicators on Child Poverty in Israel." Paper presented at the Monitoring and Measuring Children Well Being - The second international workshop, Campobasso, Italy 1997.

Hancock, Trevor. "Future Directions in Population Health." *Canadian Journal of Public Health* 90 (1999): 68-70.

Hauser, A.A. "Swedish parents don't spank." *Mothering* 63 (1992).

Hauser, Robert M., Brett V. Brown, and William R. Prosser, eds. *Indicators of children's well-being.* New York: Russell Sage Foundation, 1997.

Heller, F. "Conclusions." In *The use and abuse of social science,* edited by F. Heller, 266-281. London: Sage, 1986.

Hengst, Heinz. "Kinderarbeit revisited." *ZSE (Journal for Sociology of Education and Socialization) (German)* 98, no. 1 (1998).

Hernandez, Donald J., and Evan Charney. *From generation to generation : the health and well-being of children in immigrant families.* Washington, DC: National Academy Press, 1998.

Hobbs, Frank, and Laura Lippman. *Children's well-being : an international comparison, International population reports. Series P-95 ; no. 80.* Washington, D.C.: U.S. Dept. of Commerce Bureau of the Census, 1990.

Hodgkin, Rachel, and Peter Newell. *Implementation Handbook for the Convention on the Rights of the Child*. New-York: UNICEF, 1998.

Huebner, E.S. "Preliminary development and validation of a multidimensional life satisfaction scale of children" *Psychological Assessment*, 6: 2, (1994): 149-158.

Huebner, E.S. "Life satisfaction and happiness" In. *Children's needs II.* edited by G. Bear, K. Minke, A. 271-278. Washington: National Association of School Psychologists

Huebner, E.S., R. Gilman, and J.E. Laughlin. "A multimethod investigation of the multidimensionality of children's well-being reports: Discriminant validity of life satisfaction and self-esteem". *Social Indicators Research, 46,* (1997):1-22.

Hunter, N.D. "Testimony before the Senate committee on governmental affairs." . Washington DC: 103 US Congress, 1994.

Iezzoni, L. "Using administrative diagnostic data to assess the quality of hospital care." *International Journal of Technical Assessment in Health care* 6 (1990): 272-281.

James, Alison, and Alan Prout. "Re-presenting Childhood: Time and Transition in the Study of Childhood." In *Constructing and Reconstructing Childhood*, edited by Alison James and Alan Prout. London: Falmer Press, 1990.

Jensen, An-Magritt, and Angelo Saporiti. *Do Children Count?* Vol. 36/17, *Eurosocial report*. Vienna: European Center for Social Welfare Policy and Research, 1992.

Kadman, Yitzhack, and Miriam Gilat, eds. *Drug Addicted - New Borns (Hebrew)*. Jerusalem: National Council for the Child, 1994.

Kamerman, S.B., and A.J. Kahn. "Investing in Children: Government Expenditure for Children and their Families in Western Industrialized Countries." In *Child Poverty and Deprivation in the Industrialized Countries 1945-1995*, edited by G. A. Cornia and S. Danziger, 9l-122. Oxford: Clarendon Press, 1997.

Kretzmann, J. P., and J. L. McKnight. *Building communities from the inside out: A path toward finding and mobilizing s community's assets*. Chicago, IL: ACTA Publications., 1993.

Land, K. "Social indicators models: an overview." In *Social Indicators Models*, edited by K. Land and S. Spilerman, 5-35. New York: Russell Sage Foundation, 1975.

Larson, O., J. Doris, and W. Alvarez. "Migrants and maltreatment: Comparative evidence from central register data." *Child Abuse and Neglect* 14 (1990): 375-385.

Larson, R. M., and S. Verma. "How Children and Adolescents Spend Time Across the World: Work, Play and Developmental Opportunities" *Osychological Bulletin* 125:6 (1999): 701-736.

Lee, Bong Jo. "The Use of Census and Surveys: Implications for developing Childhood Social Indicator Models." In *Monitoring and Measuring the State of Children - Beyond Survival*, edited by Asher Ben-Arieh and Helmut Wintersberger, 301-308. Vienna: European Centre for Social Welfare Policy and Research, 1997.

Leginski, W, C Croze, J. Driggers, S. Dumpman, D. Geersten, E. Kamis-Gould, M. Namerow, R. Patton, N. Wilson, and C. Wurster. "Data Standards for Mental Health Decision Support Systems." . Washington DC: National Institute of Mental Health, DHHS, 1989.

Limber, Susan P., and Patricia Y Hashima. "An Adequate Standard of Living Necessary for Children's Cognitive Development." In *Implementing the U.N. Convention on the Rights of the Child: A standard of Living Adequate for Development*, edited by Arlene Bowers Andrews and Natalie Hevener Kaufman, 69-86. Westport, Connecticut: Prager, 1999.

Lyubomirsky, S. , and H.S. Lepper. "A Measure of Subjective Happiness: Preliminary Reliability and Construct Validation." *Social Indicators Research* 46 (1999): 137-155.

148

Masson, M., and J. Gibbs. "Patterns of Adolescent Psychiatric Hospital: Implication for Social Policy." *American Journal of Orthopsychiatry* 62 (1992): 447-457.

Melton, Gary B., and Susan Limber. "What children's rights mean to children: Children's own views." In *The ideologies of children's rights*, edited by Michel Freeman and Philip Veerman, 167-187. Dordrecht: Martinus Nijhoff, 1992.

Melton, Gary B., and Natalie Hevener Kaufman. "Monitoring of Children's Rights." In *Monitoring and Measuring the State of Children - Beyond Survival*, edited by Asher Ben-Arieh and Helmut Wintersberger, 81-88. Vienna: European Centre for Social Welfare Policy and Research, 1997.

Melton, Gary B., and M.J. Saks. "The law as an instrument of socialization and social structure." In *Nebraska Symposium on Motivation*, edited by Gary B. Melton, 235-277. Lincoln: University of Nebraska Press, 1985.

Micklewright, John, and Kitty Stewart. *Is Child Welfare Converging in the European Union.* , Florence: UNICEF International Child Development Centre, 1999.

Miles, I. *Social indicators for human development*. London: Frances Pinter, 1985.

Miljeteig, Per. "The International Effort to Monitor Children's Rights." In *Monitoring and Measuring the State of Children - Beyond Survival*, edited by Asher Ben-Arieh and Helmut Wintersberger, 55-62. Vienna: European Centre for Social Welfare Policy and Research, 1997.

Miringoff, Marc L. *The Index of Social Health 1990.* Tarrytown, NY: The Fordham Institute for Innovation in Social Policy, 1990.

Miringhoff, Marc L., and Sandra Opdycke. *The Index of Social Health: Monitoring the Social Well-being of Children in Industrialized Countries: A Report to UNICEF*. New York: The Fordham Institute for Innovation in Social Policy, 1993.

Miringoff, Marc L., Marque-Luisa Miringoff, and Sandra Opdycke. *The social health of the nation : how America is really doing*. New York: Oxford University Press, 1999.

Mondross, J.B. , and S.M. Wilson. *Organizing for power and empowerment*. New York: Columbia University Press., 1994.

Moore, Kristin A. "Criteria for Indicators of Child Well-Being." *Focus* 16, no. 3 (1995): 1-32.

Moore, Kristin A. "Criteria for Indicators of Child Well-Being." In *Indicators of children's well-being*, edited by Robert M. Hauser, Brett V. Brown and William R. Prosser, 36-44. New York: Russell Sage Foundation, 1997.

Morrow, V. "Conceptualising social capital in relation to the well-being of children and young people: a critical review." *Sociological Review* 47, no. 4 (1999): 744-765.

Mugford, M., P. Banfield, and M. O'hanlon. "Effects of feedback of information on clinical practice: a review." *British Medical Journal* 303, no. 6799 (1991): 398.

Nagy, J. & Fawcett, S.B. "VMOSA: A practical approach to strategic planning." In *Community Tool Box,*, edited by Work Group on Health Promotion and Community Development, Chap. 6, Sec. 1. Lawrence, KS: University of Kansas, 1999.

Norwegian Commissioner for Children. *Facts about Children in Norway*. Oslo: Norwegian Commissioner for Children, 1990.

Ottomanelli, Gennaro. *Children and addiction*. Westport, CT: Praeger, 1995.

Parliamentary Assembly of the Council of Europe. *Recommendation 1286 - on a European Strategy for Children.* Brussels: Council of Europe, 1996.

Percival, Richard, and Ann Harding. "The Public and Private Costs of Children In Australia, 1993-1994." Paper presented at the Conference on Child Well Being in Rich and Transition Countries, Luxembourg 1999.

Philip, Deborah, and John Love. "Indicators for school readiness, schooling and child care in early to middle childhood." In *Indicators of children's well-being*, edited by Robert M. Hauser, Brett V. Brown and William R. Prosser, 125-151. New York: Russell Sage Foundation, 1997.

Pittman, Karen, and Merita Irby. "Promoting Investment in Life Skills for Youth: Beyond Indicators for Survival and Problem Prevention." In *Monitoring and Measuring the State of Children - Beyond Survival*, edited by Asher Ben-Arieh and Helmut Wintersberger, 239-246. Vienna: European Centre for Social Welfare Policy and Research, 1997.

Plewis, I. , A. Creeser, and R. Mooney. "Reliability and validity of time budget data: children's activities outside school." *Journal of Official Statistics* 6 (1990): 411-419.

Potter, D., D. Goldblat, M. Kiloh, and P. Lewis, eds. *Democcratization*. Cambridge: Polity Press, 1997.

Prout, Alan. "Objective vs. Subjective Indicators or Both? Whose Perspective Counts?" In *Monitoring and Measuring the State of Children - Beyond Survival*, edited by Asher Ben-Arieh and Helmut Wintersberger, 89-100. Vienna: European Centre for Social Welfare Policy and Research, 1997.

Public Health Foundation. *Healthy People 2010 Toolkit*. Washington, DC: author.: Public Health Foundation, 1999.

Qvortrup, J. "Childhood Matters: An Introduction." In *Childhood Matters: Social Theory, Practice and Politics*, edited by Jens Qvortrup, Marita Brady, Giovanni Sgritta and Helmut Wintersberger. Vienna: Avebury, 1994.

Qvortrup, Jens. "From Useful to Useful: the Historical Continuity of Children's Constructive Participation." In *Sociological Studies of Children*, edited by A. Ambert. Greenwich, Con: JAI Press., 1995.

Qvortrup, Jens. "Indicators of Childhood and the Intergenerational Dimension." In *Monitoring and Measuring the State of Children - Beyond Survival*, edited by Asher Ben-Arieh and Helmut Wintersberger, 101-112. Vienna: European Center for Social Welfare Policy and Research, 1997.

Qvortrup, Jens. ""The Meaning of Child's Standard of living" In *Implementing the U.N. Convention on the Rights of the Child: A standard of Living Adequate for Development*, edited by Arlene Bowers Andrews and Natalie Hevener Kaufman, 47-57. Westport, Connecticut: Prager, 1999.

Qvortrup, Jens, Marita Brady, Giovani Sgritta, and Helmut Wintersberger, eds. *Childhood Matters: Social Theory, Practice and Politics*. Aldershot: Avebury, 1994.

Raphael, Dennis, Rebecca Renwick, Ivan Brown, and Irving Rootman. "Quality of life indicators and health: Current Status and Emerging Conceptions." *Social Indicators Research* 39 (1996): 65-88.

Renard, Roland. *Le cout de l'enfant: approches tho'oriques, methodologiques, empiriques.* Bruxelles: Minist're de la Communaut' francaise, 1985.

Resnick, M. "Discussant's Comments ." Paper presented at the Indicators of Children's Well-being. Madison WI.: Conference Papers Vol. II. 1995.

Rettig, K.D. , and R.D Leichtentritt. "A General Theory for Perceptual Indicators of Family Life Quality." *Social Indicators Research* 47 (1999): 307-342.

Rouse, Beatrice A. *Substance abuse and mental health statistics sourcebook*. Rockville, MD.: U.S. Dept. of Health and Human Services, 1995.

Rushton, Francis E., and Robert E. Greenberg. "The Relationship Between Standard of Living and Physical Development." In *An Adequate Standard of Living Necessary for Children's Cognitive Development*, edited by Arlene Bowers Andrews and Natalie Hevener Kaufman, 59-68. Westport, Connecticut: Prager, 1999.

Samuels, B., N. Ahsan, and J. Garcia. *Know your community: A step-by-step guide to community needs and resource assessment.* Chicago, IL: Family Resource Coalition, 1995.

Sauli, Hannele. "Using Databases for Monitoring the Socioeconomic State of Children." In *Monitoring and Measuring the State of Children - Beyond Survival*, edited by Asher Ben-Arieh and Helmut Wintersberger, 287-299. Vienna: European Centre for Social Welfare Policy and Research, 1997.

Shamgar-Handelman, Lea. *Childhood as a Social Phenomenon: National Report Israel.* Vol. 36/15, *Childhood as a Social Phenomenon.* Vienna: European Center for Social Welfare Policy and Research, 1990.

Sheldon, E.B., and R. Parke. "Social Indicators." *Science* 188 (1975): 693-699.

Smeeding, Timothy M., and Peter Gottschalk. *The international evidence on income distribution in modern economies : where do we stand?* Syracuse, N.Y.: Maxwell School of Citizenship and Public Affairs Syracuse University, 1995.

Smeeding, Timothy M., Michael O'Higgins, and Lee Rainwater. *Poverty, inequality, and income distribution in comparative perspective : the Luxembourg income study (LIS).* New York: Harvester Wheatsheaf, 1990.

Stoil, Michael Jon, and Gary Hill. *Preventing substance abuse : interventions that work.* New York: Plenum Press, 1996.

Straus, Murray A., and Denise A. Donnelly. *Beating the devil out of them : corporal punishment in American families.* New York: Lexington Books ;

Straus, Murray A., and Richard J. Gelles. *Physical violence in American families : risk factors and adaptations to violence in 8,145 families.* New Brunswick, N.J., U.S.A.: Transaction Publishers, 1990.

Straus, Martha B. *Violence in the lives of adolescents.* New York: Norton, 1994.

Stuhr, J.J. "Democracy as a way of life." *Kettering Review* spring (1998): 30-40.

Tardieu, Bruno. "The Human Rights of Children Growing Up in Extreme Poverty: What Lacks of Basic Securities." In *Monitoring and Measuring the State of Children - Beyond Survival*, edited by Asher Ben-Arieh and Helmut Wintersberger, 209-225. Vienna: European Centre for Social Welfare Policy and Research, 1997.

Tardieu, Bruno, Alberto Lopez, and Genevieve Defraigne Tardieu. "Impact of Indicators on Public Action Against Poverty: A Case Study." Paper presented at the Monitoring and Measuring Children Well being - The third international workshop, Kiawah resort, S.C. 1998.

Terry, T. , and E.S Huebner. "The Relationship Between Self-Concept and Life Satisfaction in Children." *Social Indicators Research* 35 (1995): 39-52.

Testa, Mark. "State comparisons of the conditions of children: The comparative state of the child project." In *Summary policy papers. What works? Intervening in the lives of at risk children*, edited by C.S. Russell and C.R. McCauley, 9-28. Nashville: Vanderbilt Institute for Public Policy Studies, 1990.

Testa, Mark, and Edward Lawlor. *The State of the Child 1985.* Chicago: Chapin Hall Center for Children at the University of Chicago, 1985.

Testa, Mark, and Fred Wulczyn. *The state of the child, A Series of research reports on children in Illinois ; v. 1.* Chicago, Ill.: Children's Policy Research Project School of Social Service Administration The University of Chicago, 1980.

Thompson, Ross A. *Preventing child maltreatment through social support : a critical analysis.* Thousand Oaks, CA: Sage Publications, 1995.

Thompson, Ross A., and Brandy Randall. "A Standard of Living Adequate for Children's Spiritual Development." In *An Adequate Standard of Living Necessary for Children's*

Cognitive Development, edited by Arlene Bowers Andrews and Natalie Hevener Kaufman, 87-104. Westport, Connecticut: Prager, 1999.

Torney-Purta, Judith, John Schwille, and Jo-Ann Amadeo, eds. *Civic Education Across Countries: Twenty-four National Case Studies from the IEA Civic Education Project.* Amsterdam: IEA, 1999.

Torney-Purta, Judith. "The Meaning of Standard of Living Adequate for Moral and Civic Development." In *Implementing the U.N. Convention on the Rights of the Child: A standard of Living Adequate for Development*, edited by Arlene Bowers Andrews and Natalie Hevener Kaufman, 105-116. Westport, Connecticut: Prager, 1999.

Touliatos, John, Barry F. Perlmutter, and Murray A. Straus. *Handbook of family measurement techniques*. Newbury Park, Calif.: Sage, 1990.

U.S. Dept. of Health and Human Services. "The feasibility of linking research-related data bases to federal and non-federal medical administrative data bases: A report to congress." . Washington DC: U.S. Dept. of Health and Human Services, 1991.

Verhellen, E. ed. *Monitoring children's rights*. The Hague. Martinus Nijhoff. 1996

Wintersberger, Helmut. "Children Costs and Benefits." In *Monitoring and Measuring the State of Children - Beyond Survival*, edited by Asher Ben-Arieh and Helmut Wintersberger, 265-274. Vienna: European Center for Social Welfare Policy and Research, 1997.

Zelizer, Viviana A. *Pricing the Priceless Child, The Changing Social Value of Children.* Princeton N.J.: Princeton University Press, 1994.

Zill, N., and Nord. C.W. "Running in place: How American families are faring in a changing economy and an individualistic society." . Washington D.C.: Child Trends, Inc., 1994.

Zill, N, H. Sigal, and O.G. Brim. "Development of childhood social indicators." In *America's unfinished business: Child and family policy*, edited by E. Zigler, S.L. Kagan and E. Klugman, 188-222. New York: Cambridge University press, 1982.

INDEX

Social Indicators Research Series

1. V. Møller (ed.): *Quality of Life in South Africa*. 1997   ISBN 0-7923-4797-8
2. G. Baechler: *Violence Through Environmental Discrimination*. Causes, Rwanda Arena, and Conflict Model. 1999   ISBN 0-7923-5495-8
3. P. Bowles and L.T. Woods (eds.): *Japan after the Economic Miracle*. In Search of New Directories. 1999   ISBN 0-7923-6031-1
4. E. Diener and D.R. Rahtz (eds.): *Advances in Quality of Life Theory and Research*. Volume I. 1999   ISBN 0-7923-6060-5
5. Kwong-leung Tang (ed.): *Social Development in Asia*. 2000   ISBN 0-7923-6256-X
6. M.M. Beyerlein (ed.): *Work Teams: Past, Present and Future*. 2000
        ISBN 0-7923-6699-9
7. A. Ben-Arieh, N.H. Kaufman, A.B. Andrews, R. Goerge, B.J. Lee, J.L. Aber (eds.): *Measuring and Monitoring Children's Well-Being*. 2001   ISBN 0-7923-6789-8

KLUWER ACADEMIC PUBLISHERS – DORDRECHT / LONDON / BOSTON